28.95

WITHDRAWN
WRIGHT STATE UNIVERSITY LIBRARIES

THE COCAINE RECOVERY BOOK

For my father

Neal N. Earley, M.D.

who leads by his example.

THE COCAINE RECOVERY BOOK

Paul H. Earley, M.D.

SAGE PUBLICATIONS
The International Professional Publishers
Newbury Park   London   New Delhi

Copyright © 1991 by Sage Publications, Inc.

All rights reserved. No part of this book may be reproduced or utilized in any form or by any means, electronic or mechanical, including photocopying, recording, or by any information storage and retrieval system, without permission in writing from the publisher.

For information address:

SAGE Publications, Inc.
2455 Teller Road
Newbury Park, California 91320

SAGE Publications Ltd.
6 Bonhill Street
London EC2A 4PU
United Kingdom

SAGE Publications India Pvt. Ltd.
M-32 Market
Greater Kailash I
New Delhi 110 048 India

Printed in the United States of America

Library of Congress Cataloging-in-Publication Data

Earley, Paul H.
  The cocaine recovery book / Paul H. Earley.
    p. cm.
  Includes bibliographical references and index.
  ISBN 0-8039-4394-6 — ISBN 0-8039-4395-4 [previously ISBN 0-926028-13-8] (pbk.)
  1. Cocaine habit. 2. Cocaine habit—Treatment. I. Title.
RC568.C6E38 1991   91-3342
616.86'47—dc 20   CIP

FIRST PRINTING, 1991

Contents

To the Cocaine User	xi
To the Professional	xiii
A Note of Caution	xvi
Organizational Notes	xvii

PART ONE
The Cocaine Addiction Cycle

Introductory Remarks	**3**
1. The History of Cocaine Use	**4**
Principles	4
2. The Complications of Cocaine Use	**13**
Principles	13
Effects on the Body	14
Oral cocaine ingestion	15
Insufflation (snorting)	15
Intravenous use	16
Freebasing or crack smoking	21
Effects on the heart and other muscles	22

Effects on the liver	23
Effects on the brain	23
Effects on the Mind	25
3. The Cocaine Addiction Cycle	**32**
Principles	32
STAGE I - Cocaine Consumption	35
STAGE II - Early Crash	38
STAGE III - Late Crash	38
STAGE IV - Between Binges	39
STAGE V - Drug Seeking	40
Additional Readings for Part One	**43**

PART TWO
The Recovery Reflex

Introductory Remarks	**47**
Principles	47
4. Detoxification	**53**
Principles	53
The Neurochemistry of Cocaine	57
Cocaine Toxicity	71

5. Cocaine Craving Patterns — 75

   Principles — 75

   Reinforced-Use Craving — 77

   Overt Interoceptive Craving — 78

   Covert Craving — 82

   Conditioned-Cue Craving — 84

6. Thought Distortion — 88

   Principles — 88

   Changes in Instincts — 89

   Denial of Cocaine Addiction — 91

   Denial of Other Facets of Addiction — 95

   Grandiosity — 97

   False Confidence — 98

   Euphoric Recall — 99

7. Mood Problems — 103

   Principles — 103

   The First Week of Abstinence — 104

   The pink cloud — 106

   Cocaine-Induced Depression — 107

Affect-Oriented Psychotherapy	108
Grief	108
Anger	109
Loneliness	110
Sadness	111
8. The Twelve Steps	**113**
Principles	113
Step One	115
Step Two	118
Step Three	120
After the First Three Steps	122
Welcome to recovery!	123
9. Relapse Prevention	**124**
Principles	124
Event-Based Relapse Prevention	127
Behavioral techniques	128
Cognitive techniques	132
Lifestyle changes	134

The Process Model of Relapse	137
The components of relapse	139
A relapse example	141
Points of intervention in the process model	144
Drug Screening in Recovery	146
10. Long-Term Therapy and Cocaine	**148**
Principles	148
Eating Disorders	152
Difficulties with Intimacy	154
Sexual Addiction	156
Emotional Cycling	158
The Oscillating Ego	160
Success/Failure Complex	161
Restless Inner Self	166
Additional Readings for Part Two	**169**
Index	**171**
About the Author	**189**

Figures and Tables

List of Figures

1. Timeline of Cocaine Use	6
2. How Fast Does Cocaine Affect the Brain?	9
3. The Cocaine Addiction Cycle	34
4. Stage Switching in the Cocaine Addiction Cycle	37
5. A Neuron	56
6. The Synapse Between Two Neurons	57
7. The Effect of Cocaine on the Synapse	59
8. Periods of Mood Problems in Early Recovery	105
9. The Process Model of Relapse Prevention	138
10. Points of Intervention to Prevent Relapse	143

List of Tables

1. Primary Medications in Cocaine Detoxification	65
2. Secondary Medications in Cocaine Detoxification	69
3. The Components of Cocaine Brain Toxicity	72
4. The Four Types of Cocaine Craving	77

To the Cocaine User

(and Those Who Care About a Cocaine User)

You may have picked up this book thinking, "Maybe this will help me stop cocaine." Or you may have picked it up thinking it would be helpful for a friend or loved one who has problems with cocaine. If all you are willing to do is read a book about addiction and no more—STOP—do not buy this book. The Cocaine Recovery Book is not a do-it-yourself book. However, if you are willing to learn about cocaine addiction and do what is necessary to help yourself or a loved one recover from addiction, then this book is for you.

The Cocaine Recovery Book is intended to educate and to promote change. If you have a clear understanding of the development of your cocaine addiction and the effect cocaine has on your body, your mind, and your life, you will reinforce your determination to stop. When you understand the process of healing from cocaine addiction, you will be better prepared to fight the battle of recovery.

Education should not be confused with treatment. Knowing about cocaine addiction will not stop you or your loved one from using. Some type of group or individual treatment is almost always necessary. If you or your loved one is smoking or injecting cocaine, I recommend an intensive, organized treatment program. Treatment programs interrupt the destructive downhill spiral of cocaine use. I know I could not have done it alone. I strongly urge you to seek help too.

When you or your loved one begins treatment, you will face major challenges—challenges that will continue for the first year of recovery. This book describes the problems and offers solutions to most problems facing the recovering addict. The most difficult problem you will have is allowing change. Change is hard work—it requires a strong commitment. As difficult as it is to stop using cocaine, stopping cocaine is *not* recovery. Change is the real work of recovery. Recovery involves changing your perceptions and beliefs about most everything in life.

Before beginning treatment, you should carefully examine your motivation to stop using. Do you want to cut down or stop completely? Use only on weekends? Continue to use socially? Research in addictive disease demonstrates that cocaine is a powerfully addictive drug. When a person is dependent on cocaine, he will be *unable* to return to casual cocaine use. The goal of addiction treatment is to end your drug use altogether and enter recovery.

How then can you tell if you or a loved one is dependent on cocaine—a cocaine addict? You are addicted if your cocaine use has caused trouble in your emotional, social, financial, or spiritual life—on any level. You are addicted if your friends have expressed concern, *especially* if you thought they were blowing it out of proportion. Most people have an image in their minds of what a cocaine addict is and, at first, most addicts believe that they don't fit the description. If you think you may have a problem, the chances are you do!

Early in recovery you or your loved one must also examine your use of alcohol and other drugs. The majority of cocaine addicts are cross-addicted—most commonly to alcohol or other drugs. Cocaine addicts are often involved in addictive relationships or engage in other compulsive behaviors. From the start, I urge you to be open to examine all aspects of your addictive illness.

To the Professional

The Cocaine Recovery Book is an educational text about cocaine dependence and recovery. Physicians, psychologists, social workers, and addiction therapists will all deepen their understanding of cocaine dependence by reading this book; it provides information for every professional who treats addiction. *The Cocaine Recovery Book* does not provide case studies of successfully recovered addicts, preach recovery, or review all the scientific literature for all possible treatment methods. Rather, this book will assist you in your day-to-day work with patients, detailing the step-by-step procedure an addict must take to extricate himself from the tangled web of cocaine addiction.

The Cocaine Recovery Book helps addicts understand their addiction as a deep-seated cycle of binge cocaine use, remorse, and denial—not simply the result of too much cocaine. The text outlines the physical and psychological consequences of cocaine use. Knowing this information will help dislodge the addict's denial and minimization of his illness.

You will learn how cocaine affects the brain and that many of the addict's behaviors are a direct consequence of the toxic effects of cocaine on the brain. Addicts undergo specific periods of mood changes and drug craving. *The Cocaine Recovery Book* will teach you how to assist the recovering patient during these difficult times. This book describes extensive relapse-prevention techniques and details specific maneuvers that cocaine addicts should employ to ensure continued sobriety.

Most professionals find that cocaine addicts have an insatiable appetite for information about addiction. At the same time, most cocaine addicts hide their feelings behind walls of intellectualization and rationalization; they use these defenses to avoid feeling the desperation that results from their addiction. *The Cocaine Recovery Book* provides the needed information, but at the same time prompts the addict to change. Information about the past consequences of addiction is always presented along with methods for change in his recovery. This book uses the addict's curiosity as a tool to effect change, and avoids harsh confrontation of the addict's tendency to intellectualize his plight. An addict's primary mode of defense against change thus becomes his deepest ally in providing the basis for an emotional and cognitive shift—into recovery.

The Cocaine Recovery Book is divided into two parts. Part One describes the development of cocaine addiction and the medical and psychological consequences of being addicted. Part Two, which comprises the bulk of this book, addresses recovery. Grounded in the principles of twelve-step recovery, Part Two depicts the reflexive change that occurs when addicts become drug-free, work to resolve their pasts, and participate in a program of recovery. Part Two lays out a complete road map of the first year of recovery.

Once you become familiar with the book, you may wish to direct your patients to read certain chapters and complete the corresponding exercises in *The Cocaine Recovery Workbook* as part of their treatment. Exercises in the companion workbook help the addict to pace himself and reinforce the major concepts of each chapter. After an addict has read and understood Chapter Three, the remaining chapters in this book can be read in any order. Each chapter begins with a list of principles that guide the reading and direct the exercises in the workbook. You may also find these principles helpful to use as focal points for discussion in education or therapy groups.

Although most cocaine addicts will benefit from reading this book, it is not designed to be an addict's only source of information. The essence of twelve-step recovery is best obtained from *Alcoholics Anonymous*, the A.A. "Big Book", *Twelve Steps and Twelve Traditions*, and *Narcotics Anonymous*, the "Blue Book".

Almost all cocaine addicts suffer from multiple manifestations of their addictive disease. The most common co-manifestation is alcoholism. To recover, the cocaine addict must examine his use of alcohol and other drugs, as well as any compulsive or destructive behaviors that may compound his disease. Some addicts enter treatment fully cognizant of the other facets of their addiction. Others need time in recovery before they are able to see the secondary symptoms of their addiction. *The Cocaine Recovery Book* focuses on cocaine without discounting other addictions. Although it is important for professionals to point out to their patients any concomitant addictive behaviors, I recommend that power struggles over such issues be avoided during early recovery. In time, most cocaine addicts appreciate that their addiction has many forms, and that cocaine use was simply the most obvious manifestation of their addictive disease.

At the end of Parts One and Two you will find a selective reading list. The references in this list are by no means exhaustive, but are intended to enlarge on the concepts presented in this text. I hope you will find that *The Cocaine Recovery Book* expands the horizon of your work with people in recovery.

A Note of Caution

Before anyone begins reading this book, I feel it is necessary to give a word of caution.

If you are in the early stage of recovery from cocaine addiction (the first six months), you should pay close attention to cues from your body while you read. Cocaine programs the mind with powerful memories. Most recovering addicts find that simply reading and thinking about their experiences with cocaine produces craving for the drug.

Cocaine craving may start in many ways. You may feel your heart racing, your stomach churning, or a cold sweat breaking out on your hands or other parts of your body. If you feel cravings while reading this book or any other recovery literature, *stop reading and talk to someone about the cravings.* Do not push them away. On the other hand, be careful not to embellish the cravings or keep them alive. The cravings will go away, if you don't use.

Chapter Five in Part Two of this book discusses more about cocaine craving as well as techniques for handling the craving. In the meantime, read as much as possible without getting anxious. It will do no good to push through the reading of this book if it only makes you uncomfortable.

Why would cocaine cravings be generated by reading about the destruction of cocaine addiction? This is one of the many paradoxes of cocaine dependence. Read on to learn more.

Organizational Notes

Each chapter in this book begins with a set of principles that guide the reading and direct the exercises in the companion workbook. It is best to read each principle, think about it for a moment, and then read the text. Once each chapter is completed, review the principles again to ensure that you understand the main points.

If you are using *The Cocaine Recovery Workbook,* complete the corresponding workbook exercises as you finish your reading of each chapter in the main text. Your therapist or physician may be interested in your responses to these exercises. As you read, you may wish to take note of the reference list at the end of Parts One and Two for additional reading material.

Although there is a great deal of valuable information in *The Cocaine Recovery Book,* it is only one of many valuable sources of information. A minimum reading list should include the following:

- *Alcoholics Anonymous,* the A.A. "Big Book"
- *Twelve Steps and Twelve Traditions*
- *Narcotics Anonymous,* the "Blue Book"

Use these books as guides to twelve-step recovery.

Please understand that cocaine is very toxic to the brain and, although you or a loved one may deny it, a cocaine-toxic brain will distort, misinterpret, and be unable to comprehend parts of any text. If you have recently stopped your drug use, you may find it helpful at times to reread chapters and redo exercises to gain the full benefit from these books.

Throughout this book I have chosen to use the pronoun *he* to refer to both men and women. The use of the male pronoun is not meant to imply that cocaine addiction only occurs in men. Nor do I mean to offend women by using the male pronoun exclusively. If you or your loved one is a female addict, substitute *she* for *he* when it occurs in the text.

As you begin *The Cocaine Recovery Book,* read slowly and thoroughly, examine the feelings that arise, try to be honest, and talk with others about what you have read and experienced. Remember, recovery from cocaine addiction is not a race. If you have *The Cocaine Recovery Workbook,* begin the first exercise now. Then move on to Part One.

PART ONE

The Cocaine Addiction Cycle

Introductory Remarks

Part One of this book begins by describing the history of cocaine use. The historical information in Chapter One describes the long relationship man has had with cocaine. History teaches us that the route by which cocaine is consumed contributes to the severity of the cocaine problem. Using this information, we will learn why cocaine addiction is a problem today.

Part One then reviews the effects of cocaine on the body and introduces some of the effects of cocaine on the mind. Cocaine is toxic to both the body and the mind. Chapter Two is a guide to many of the complications that occur during and as a result of cocaine addiction. Reading Chapter Two will not scare anyone into stopping their cocaine use. No one has stopped consuming cocaine because he read that cocaine is not good for him. Rather, Chapter Two is an inventory of the many effects that cocaine has on the body and mind.

Part One concludes with a description of the Cocaine Addiction Cycle. Most cocaine addicts use in a cyclic pattern that confuses them into believing that their cocaine use is not as bad as it seems, or even that they have no true addiction at all. When an addict understands the Cocaine Addiction Cycle, he will be able to extract himself from this powerful cycle. Chapter Three may ignite cocaine craving. Cocaine users should read this chapter carefully and under supervision.

ONE

The History of Cocaine Use

Principles

1. Social, economic, and cultural factors generated the current cocaine epidemic.

2. The current cocaine epidemic is fueled by a pure drug consumed by very addicting routes of administration.

3. Cocaine euphoria and, therefore, addiction are created by a change in drug level in the brain rather than the actual level of the drug in the body.

Cocaine and cocaine alkaloids, extracted from two coca plant species *Erythroxylon coca* and *Erythroxylon novogranatense*, have been used by man since 800 A.D. It was first cultivated by cultures that predated the Incan Empire. In the early Incan culture, coca use occurred at all levels of society. Use of the coca plant shifted from common use to religious ritual with the rise of the Incan Empire. Coca was harvested by the Incas as part of their religious practice and consumed by tribal leaders. During the height of the empire, the use of coca leaves was restricted to official uses by soldiers, priests, and nobility.

As the power of the Incas faded, cocaine use returned to the masses. The Spaniards, who invaded Peru in the 1500s, reported that cocaine chewing was commonplace. Although the Catholic Church attempted to eliminate coca chewing, they soon found the enslaved South American Indians poorly motivated without cocaine. Eventually, the church reinstated coca chewing to the Indians in a pragmatic attempt to increase the output of the native Incan slave labor.

The Incan culture chewed raw leaves to obtain the active compounds in the coca leaf. Historical data from this time described the Indians placing several leaves in the mouth with an alkaline plug. The plug, due to its alkaline nature, helped extract cocaine and many related psychoactive alkaloids from the leaf. Once these compounds were extracted from the leaf, they were swallowed into the stomach. The cocaine was absorbed into the bloodstream from the stomach and small intestine much like food. Because the cocaine was eaten, it took time to be absorbed into the bloodstream and to pass to the organ of effect, the brain. Consumed in this manner, orally ingested (eaten) cocaine takes twenty minutes to be felt by the brain. The level in the bloodstream rises slowly and remains stable during any given period of cocaine chewing.

The South American Indians of the 1500s (and the millions of coca chewing Indians today) felt mild stimulation, a reduction in their appetite, and increased energy. When eaten, cocaine also produces a mild elevation in body temperature, a mild increase in the heart rate (tachycardia), and an increase in movement (motor activity). Note that there is no intense excitement or euphoria and less post-cocaine crash than is felt by modern cocaine snorters, shooters, and smokers.

After the invasion of Peru by the Spaniards, cocaine was brought back to western culture in the 1600s. The plant was classified at this time by European botanists, but drew little attention until the 1800s. The drug cocaine was isolated from the coca leaf by a physician, Albert Nieman, in the 1860s. The first literature on the physical and psychological effects of cocaine was published in several works by Sigmund Freud in the 1880s. The largest of these works was *Uber Coca*, which described the euphoric, antidepressant, and antifatigue effects of the drug. *Uber Coca* was based on physiologic and psychologic experiments; Freud self-administered cocaine, and documented extensive information about the drug's effects. This manuscript remained the definitive dissertation on the effects of cocaine on humans until the 1970s. Freud also promoted the drug as a cure for morphinism (morphine addiction). Due to increasing reports of cocaine addiction, Freud quietly withdrew his support for the use of cocaine in the late 1800s.

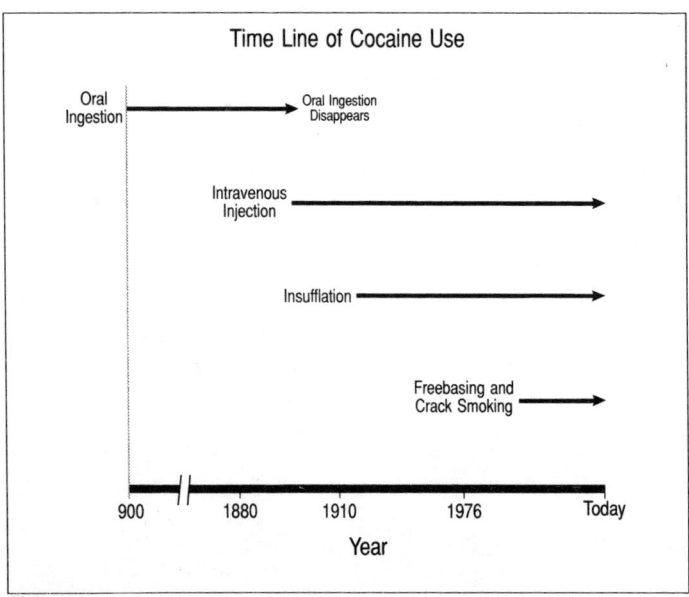

Figure 1
As cocaine use has spread, the route of consumption has shifted from eating and snorting to crack smoking and cocaine shooting.

Once discovered by western culture, cocaine quickly became one of the favored ingredients in the patent medicine industry of the 1890s. Cocaine-containing medicines produced at the turn of the century were promoted for every conceivable ailment from headaches to hair loss. One such tonic, Vin Marinari, was endorsed by many celebrities, including the pope, as a *refreshing elixir*. Cocaine even found its way into Coca-Cola, the famous tonic developed around the turn of the century in Atlanta, Georgia. Coca-Cola was first promoted as a nonalcoholic medicinal tonic, not a refreshing beverage. The Coca-Cola Company soon discovered the side effects of the cocaine in its tonic. In 1903, the cocaine in Coca-Cola was replaced by another stimulant, caffeine.

When cocaine was used in this form, a relatively low rate of addiction occurred. Although abuse, addiction, and toxicity were reported, cocaine-containing tonics could be consumed without the overwhelming consequences we see in today's cocaine-using society. This difference in the incidence of severe addiction is important. It indicates that orally ingested cocaine might be accompanied by a lower biologic incidence of addiction. Why is this? Read on.

In the early 1900s, cocaine powder was available in some social circles. This powder was snorted much like snuff. Reports from this time describe pockets of cocaine addiction mostly among upper class individuals in England and the United States. Cocaine was also used by intravenous injection during this time. A small segment of the population began injecting the drug and found it to be very addictive. It appeared that the probability of cocaine consumption becoming cocaine addiction was correlated with how cocaine was used: the lowest incidence of addiction occurring in those who ate the drug, higher in those who snorted the drug, and highest in those people who used cocaine by intravenous injection.

Problems in the patent medicine industry and outbreaks of cocaine addiction during the turn of the century led to the first national restriction of drug trade, the Pure Food and Drug Act of 1906. The Pure Food and Drug Act of 1906 was followed by the Harrison Act of 1914. The Harrison Act required companies and individuals who traded in drugs classified as narcotics (primarily cocaine and morphine) to register their activities with the Internal Revenue Service. Then, in 1922, the Narcotic Drug Import and Export Act restricted the importation of coca leaves to medicinal uses. The medical disease of addiction was managed by legislation. Cocaine use went underground, but allusions to its aphrodisiac and powerful effects on the mind continued in music and literature. The term *dope fiend* was coined in this era, partially to describe the cocaine addict.

Principle 1 — Social, economic, and cultural factors generated the current cocaine epidemic.

It wasn't until the 1960s that cocaine became readily available again. Four distinct factors contributed to the rising popularity of cocaine in the 1960s and its rise to epidemic use in the 1970s.

The first factor was cocaine's reputation when snorted. It was touted as safe, nonaddictive, and fun. Medical textbooks from the 1960s described cocaine as a nonaddicting drug. This reputation led to increased experimental consumption. The performing arts portrayed the use of cocaine in social situations without harsh consequences. Glamorous people of Hollywood seemed to be using cocaine for fun. Cocaine's reputation as a drug to use at parties grew.

The second factor was the cost of cocaine. Cocaine was expensive. At first, it was only used by those who could afford it. Cocaine was tied to the upper socioeconomic classes. This upper class status produced a new image and removed the social stigma attached to cocaine in the 1920s. The expense of cocaine added to its glamour; the glamour, in turn, promoted cocaine consumption. In the 1970s, cocaine's popularity grew. Cocaine was associated with wealth and power. Sadly, much of cocaine's status as a drug of the elite remains today despite its heavy use by those in impoverished areas and its association with ghetto crime organizations. Paradoxically, the high cost of cocaine increased its availability and its consumption.

The third factor that promoted cocaine use was the rise of the counterculture during the 1960s. Cocaine became available at the tail end of this decade, when the drug movement had redefined what was normal. Drug abuse was becoming the norm in the 1960s. Phrases like "Better living through chemistry" made the use of illicit drugs seem acceptable. Our society was primed to consume drugs, and cocaine swept through our drug using society.

The fourth factor behind the cocaine epidemic was the profitability of selling cocaine. Because cocaine was expensive, small, and easily transportable, it was also profitable. The black market for marijuana was well formed, and cocaine rewarded marijuana dealers with a higher return on their investment. This drove more drug dealers to sell cocaine, who spread its popularity into new markets. As cocaine dealing has grown, its market focus has shifted. The current drug market has expanded and migrated from a casual circle of friends making consensual drug purchases to the urban ghetto, where crack dealers sell drugs on the corner.

Each of these four factors combined in a synergistic way to produce the cocaine epidemic of the 1970s. A fifth, biologic factor added fuel to the burning fire of the epidemic.

The History of Cocaine Use

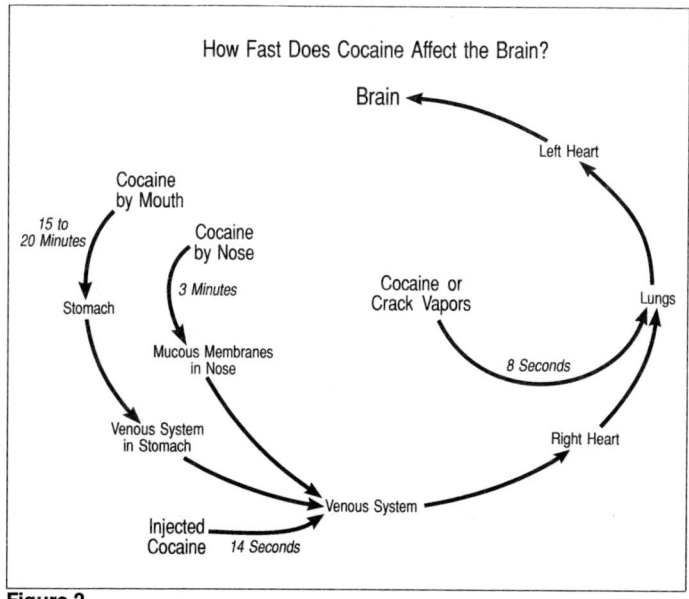

Figure 2
The method of administration determines the speed of the drug's effect on the brain: eating (20 min.), snorting (3 min.), shooting (14 sec.), or smoking (8 sec.). The more efficient the means of administration, the greater the potential for addiction.

Principle 2 — The current cocaine epidemic is fueled by a pure drug consumed by very addicting routes of administration.

Throughout the history of cocaine use, man has found more and more effective means of delivering cocaine to the brain. When cocaine is eaten, it takes fifteen to twenty minutes to reach the brain. When eaten, much of the drug is not absorbed from the stomach. When the drug is insufflated (snorted), it moves to the brain in three to four minutes. Some of the cocaine remains in the nasal passages and is not absorbed into the body. When cocaine is injected, it arrives at the brain in fourteen *seconds*. When injected, the body receives all of the cocaine directly into its bloodstream. Whether eaten, snorted, or injected cocaine is distributed through the entire venous system, which dilutes its effect on the brain.

In the early 1970s, cocaine users began converting the commonly available cocaine hydrochloride salt into a form that was first known as *base*, but is now known as *crack* or *crack cocaine*. This form of cocaine can be smoked or vaporized, delivering it to the brain in less than eight seconds. When freebase or crack is smoked, it is well absorbed. Furthermore, because crack is absorbed into the blood supply of the lungs, it is not diluted in the venous part of the blood system, but remains concentrated in arterial blood on its first trip to the brain. This gives the crack smoker an extremely fast, high dose of cocaine, administered directly to the brain. Crack smokers are rarely using a more pure form of cocaine. They are simply delivering a concentrated blast of the drug as quickly as possible to the brain. Crack or base smoking is the most addictive way to use cocaine. Why is this? Simply stated, the euphoric and addictive qualities of cocaine seem to be directly related to how fast the drug is delivered to the brain. Cocaine users migrate from eating and snorting toward smoking and shooting cocaine to increase the speed and quantity of cocaine that reaches the brain.

Principle 3 — Cocaine euphoria and, therefore, addiction are created by a change in drug level in the brain rather than the actual level of the drug in the body.

When the cocaine reaches the brain, it floods the reward center in the brain. The massive reward sensation creates euphoria, the high the addict desires. The brain quickly adjusts to the flooding of the reward center by dramatically decreasing its response to further cocaine stimulation. If an addict continues to use cocaine, he senses less and less euphoria with each subsequent dose. The maximum euphoria occurs during a change in the drug level, not during a steady state of cocaine intoxication. The faster the transition from a no-drug or a low-drug level to a higher level, the harder it is for the brain to adjust to the presence of cocaine. The transition creates the reward. The brain's inability to compensate for the cocaine effect further promotes this reward sensation. The intensity of the reward trains the brain to seek more drug. In an individual who is prone to develop addiction, this entrainment drives the occasional cocaine user to become an addict. The stronger the sensation of reward is in a person, the more powerful is the drive to use more cocaine. Smoking crack or injecting cocaine produces the strongest reward and, therefore, the strongest addiction potential of any drug known to mankind.

Cocaine addicts rarely enjoy the effects of cocaine after the initial rush. They feel the onset of euphoria, but this is quickly followed by agitation, paranoia, restlessness, and dysphoria (the opposite of euphoria). Unlike other drug users, the cocaine user does not use cocaine to feel the sustained effect of the drug on his body. Instead, most cocaine addicts use to "get off"—to experience the rush of the initial cocaine euphoria. Cocaine addicts spend their using time trying to recapture past remembrances of a previous cocaine rush. When the addict feels distressed, his brain remembers the past reward; this memory drives him to use more. The more intense the past euphoria, the stronger the drive to recapture the high with another hit of cocaine. Much of an addict's journey into addiction is paved with the intention of recapturing a few times when using cocaine produced great pleasure.

The cocaine epidemic has increased in its fury as man has moved from eating and snorting to injecting and smoking cocaine. Cocaine snorters frequently progress to cocaine dependence. The brain is entrained by the cocaine reward to continue to use cocaine. On the other hand, the experimental crack smoker or cocaine injector, because of how he uses the drug, creates a more intense euphoria and entrainment, and therefore has an overwhelming probability of becoming an addict. The number of first time crack smokers continues to rise. This accounts for the biologic drive of the current cocaine epidemic.

Now, in the 1990s, we are in the mature stages of a prolonged cocaine epidemic. Cocaine moved from an experimental drug of the 1960s to a drug of the elite in the early 1970s. From the elite, it spread in the 1980s to become a mainstream sociologic and psychologic problem. It is estimated that twenty-five million Americans have used cocaine. Three million of them are addicted. When one begins using cocaine casually, he has no intentions of becoming a statistic. However, cocaine creates a stereotypical downhill course that ends in physical, emotional, social, and spiritual problems. Cocaine pushes casual users to become statistics. This book should be part of an addict's efforts to reverse this downhill course, to recapture life.

TWO

The Complications of Cocaine Use

Principles

1. Some side effects of cocaine use are specific to the route of administration.

2. Cocaine use spreads viral illnesses such as hepatitis and AIDS.

3. Of all the organs in the body, cocaine is most toxic to the brain.

4. Each one of us is unique; however, cocaine addiction reduces us to cocaine-using animals.

Cocaine is directly toxic to the body and powerfully toxic to the brain. I will first describe the complications of cocaine use specific to the route of administration. Then, I will delineate the toxic effects of cocaine on the body's organs. The heart, the brain, and the liver each have specific responses to cocaine-induced injury. Finally, this chapter will present how cocaine affects the mind. Laboratory research on animals describes how cocaine affects the animal brain. This research will help the reader understand the effects of cocaine on the animal part of the human brain and how this guides our thoughts and feelings.

Effects on the Body

In Chapter One, we learned about the various methods by which cocaine has been used in the past and today. Cocaine is used by any or all of these four methods:

- **Oral ingestion.** Cocaine is absorbed by the stomach and other parts of the gastrointestinal tract. Once absorbed, cocaine enters the bloodstream and is carried on to the brain in about twenty minutes.
- **Insufflation (snorting).** The drug is inhaled into the nose. Once in the nose, cocaine adheres to the mucous membrane (a type of highly permeable skin inside the nose). It crosses the mucous membrane of the nose and enters the bloodstream. The cocaine travels in the bloodstream to the brain in about three minutes.
- **Intravenous usage.** The drug is injected directly into the bloodstream. Once in the bloodstream, the drug is transported to the brain in as little as fourteen seconds.
- **Crack smoking or freebase smoking.** The drug is vaporized by heat and inhaled into the lungs. Once in the lungs, the vapors move down the passageways of the lungs and into the alveoli. The alveoli are very small sacks that extract oxygen from the air. Cocaine vapors are absorbed with oxygen into the lungs' blood supply. From there, the drug moves to the left heart, and finally to the brain—all in less than eight seconds.

Principle 1 — Some side effects of cocaine use are specific to the route of administration.

Cocaine that is eaten, snorted, and injected always finds its way to the venous blood supply. It must travel from the venous system to the right chamber of the heart, then through the lungs, and then into the left heart. It is ejected with the blood from the left heart into the arterial system. Twenty percent of the output from the left heart is sent to the brain. Cocaine then crosses the blood-brain barrier on its way to the brain. The blood-brain barrier is a selective barrier that allows only certain compounds to cross from the bloodstream into the brain. Once across the blood-brain barrier cocaine enters the organ of effect, the brain.

Crack or freebase cocaine is vaporized in the pipe and quickly enters the lungs. Crack cocaine has the most direct route to the brain and, unlike cocaine that is eaten, snorted, or injected, it remains concentrated in arterial blood on its first pass to the brain. This accounts for crack's rapid onset and intense effect on the brain and its potential to create addiction.

Each route of administration has its unique side effects, so I will discuss each one separately.

Oral cocaine ingestion

Oral ingestion of cocaine has been associated with gastric and duodenal ulcers. Cocaine smugglers consume plastic bags or condoms filled with cocaine (cocaine body packing) and travel with the cocaine inside their bodies. Frequently, the bags or condoms burst, leaking the cocaine into their intestines. These unfortunate people have often overdosed and died from the cocaine they have absorbed. One *can* die from eating cocaine.

Insufflation (snorting)

Insufflation or cocaine snorting damages the delicate lining on the inside of the nose and nasal passages. Cocaine has a powerful constricting effect on the small blood vessels that supply vital nutrients to our tissues. When cocaine is consumed repeatedly, this frequent constriction of the blood vessels in the nose decreases the blood supply to the mucous membranes that line the inner passages in the sinuses and nose. The decreased blood supply to the mucous membranes causes sections of the membranous tissue in the nose to die. This localized necrosis (death) of tissue produces holes in the delicate turbinates or the septum of the nose. Individuals who snort the drug routinely develop nose bleeds, sinus problems, and infections. Over the years, continued cocaine snorting has been reported to cause necrosis of the dividing walls within the nose. As pieces of the walls die, holes form in these walls. The most common hole occurs in the septum, the major wall between the right and left sides of the nose. Corrective surgery is sometimes necessary.

If the nasal passages become infected, antibiotics are used to prevent the infection from spreading from the nose to the nasal sinuses and the brain.

Intravenous use

The intravenous use of any drug is fraught with complications. Intravenous injection produces complications primarily from the use of unsterile needles and impure drugs. Even if a drug addict uses sterile needles, the cocaine itself is not sterile. Addicts may dissolve cocaine in sterile water hoping to reduce the health risk of using. The end result, however, is a unsterile solution. This cocaine solution creates frequent health problems. All addicts who inject cocaine introduce bacteria into the body. The bacteria in the cocaine or the unsterile needles can implant themselves on the valves of the heart or create a pocket of bacterial growth in the brain or the lungs. These small collections of bacteria damage vital organs, including the heart valves, and may create infections or balls of pus in the brain, kidneys, and lungs.

An infection in the valves of the heart is called endocarditis. Endocarditis endangers the heart's pumping action by damaging the heart's valves—causing the heart to fail. Addicts may require heart surgery to replace damaged heart valves. If the infection lodges in the brain, seizures and death may result. If the infection lands in the kidneys, one's fluid balance may become upset, and kidney function may fail. If the body is unable to fight off the infection caused by the introduction of only a few bacteria, the body becomes septic as bacteria grow through the bloodstream. This type of sepsis is often fatal.

Principle 2 — Cocaine use spreads viral illnesses such as hepatitis and AIDS.

The use of intravenous needles is also associated with an alarming incidence of transmission of many viruses, including

HIV—the virus that is responsible for AIDS. These viruses are carried from drug user to drug user by shared syringes, cocaine, or through sexual transmission.

One of these viruses is the hepatitis virus. Three identified types of liver viruses are commonly transmitted by needles. These are called hepatitis A, hepatitis B, and hepatitis C. Hepatitis A can be transmitted through the air, but hepatitis B and C are transmitted most frequently through sharing needles or intravenous solutions. Hepatitis B is also transmitted through intimate sexual contact with a carrier of the hepatitis B virus.

Hepatitis causes liver inflammation which can lead to liver failure. Symptoms of hepatitis include nausea, vomiting, and a lack of energy or motivation. As the liver becomes compromised, it cannot metabolize (process) certain chemicals. This causes mental confusion, lethargy, seizures, and even respiratory failure. One chemical, bilirubin, is processed in the liver and excreted from the body in the feces. When one develops hepatitis, bilirubin is not removed from the blood and is subsequently deposited in the skin, causing it to turn yellow. The excess bilirubin in the bloodstream also turns the whites of the eyes deep yellow. Hepatitis B and C can produce permanent liver damage. Vaccines prevent one from getting hepatitis, but no known medication helps the body fight the hepatitis viruses once they enter the body. Hepatitis is best treated with rest, proper diet, and abstinence from drugs and alcohol. Even when one recovers from the hepatitis infection, he may carry the hepatitis virus in his body and spread the infection to others.

If a drug user develops hepatitis B or C, it may lead to a chronically inflamed or cirrhotic liver. This type of liver inflammation is caused by the body's response to the hepatitis virus. The compromised liver causes a chronic illness with fatigue, food intolerance, and confusion. Medications are rarely helpful in treating liver inflammation or chronic cirrhosis.

An intravenous drug user should talk to his physician. Ask the physician if a viral hepatitis panel or profile should be drawn along with other laboratory studies while in treatment. The panel is a simple blood test. If one has had a history of a long flu-like illness, and especially if he has "turned yellow," he should determine if he has been exposed to the hepatitis viruses. If anyone has been exposed to hepatitis, it is his *obligation* to discover if he has become a virus carrier and therefore could infect others. It is the ethical obligation of every hepatitis carrier to learn about safe sex practices and how not to spread the disease to others.

In recent times, a more ominous virus has been discovered among intravenous drug users, the Human Immunodeficiency Virus (HIV), the causative agent in Acquired Immunodeficiency Syndrome (AIDS). First associated in the United States with homosexual men, the second largest group of HIV infected individuals are intravenous drug users, most of whom shoot cocaine. These two groups illustrate the two major routes for the spread of HIV. The first route is sexual transmission. Individuals who are sexually active with multiple partners transmit the virus through many forms of intimate sexual contact. A second route of transmission is through the intravenous use of cocaine and other drugs. Needle sharing is the fastest rising cause of the spread of AIDS.

HIV requires a very delicate transport medium from person to person to survive. Extracting blood (even a minute amount) from one user and injecting this blood into someone else is indeed a good transport medium, and the most direct method of transmitting AIDS. Other methods of sharing blood or semen can transmit HIV. Once a person is infected, the virus may generate a short-lived, flu-like syndrome with a mild fever, rash, and muscle pains (myalgias). Infection with HIV may be associated with no immediate problems, however. The virus may remain dormant for six months or more. When the HIV becomes active, it suppresses the body's immune system. This prevents the body from fighting off simple infections. AIDS patients develop signs of the spread of the virus throughout the body. These include recurrent infections (often with unusual organisms) and body wasting. HIV keeps the body from fighting cancer as well. One form of cancer, Kaposi's sarcoma, has become commonplace among AIDS victims. Kaposi's sarcoma was once a rare illness of elderly men in certain ethnic groups. At present, Kaposi's sarcoma seems to occur among homosexual AIDS victims, rarely in intravenous drug-using AIDS patients. However, other forms of cancer, including lymphoma and leukemia, occur in drug-abusing AIDS patients. Because AIDS patients have a massively suppressed immune system, they commonly die of pneumonia or other infections. Late in the development of HIV disease, patients suffer from dementia (a continual confusion state).

The AIDS test is called an HIV antibody titre. The confirmation test for HIV exposure is the Western Blot. Who should have the HIV antibody titre? Two categories of people should have the AIDS test: IV drug users and those who have been sexually promiscuous. Anyone who has used needles outside a medical setting should consider having an AIDS test. Many cocaine addicts cannot remember whether they have shared needles or not. Intending to be clean in his needle usage, an IV cocaine user will begin cocaine use and, in a frenzy, abandon his ritual for insuring that he uses a clean needle or syringe. Therefore, all IV cocaine users should consider having the HIV titre drawn. Anyone who has been sexually active with multiple partners should consider having the HIV titre drawn as well. It is easy to practice safe sex. However, individuals who have sex with many partners rarely use condoms and other safe practices one hundred percent of the time. If one is unsure, he should learn whether or not he has been exposed to HIV.

Before an HIV antibody titre is drawn, a physician or trained counselor should discuss the medical, social, and ethical consequences of having the testing done. The decision to draw an HIV antibody titre should be an informed one. The physician or counselor should discuss the consequences of a positive test, the accuracy and the meaning of a false positive (the extremely rare occurrence of an HIV antibody titre returning positive, when no true HIV is present), and the meaning of a false negative (the HIV antibody titre returning negative, when HIV is present in the body). This test should never be done casually due to the extreme consequences of either a positive or negative test.

When the test results are positive, the patient will need further evaluation and treatment. Drug-using friends and sex partners should be contacted by the patient or his physician or counselor to inform them of the test results. If the HIV antibody test is positive, the patient must actively seek treatment for HIV exposure and his addiction right away. A negative HIV antibody titre indicates that one has not been exposed to the HIV, but many people exposed to HIV remain seronegative (test negative on the HIV antibody test) for twelve months or more. The HIV antibody titre says nothing about recent exposure to the virus. Therefore, a negative HIV antibody titre does not completely rule out AIDS or whether someone is capable of transmitting HIV to others. For these and other reasons, I teach safe sexual practices to *all* patients under my care. Please note that treatment programs may have procedures that differ from those I have outlined above. None of us, however, can try to look the other way and hope AIDS will just go away. Note as well that this book should not be used as a sole source of information about AIDS. If the reader has further questions, please refer to *Additional Readings* at the end of Part One.

The injection of drugs into the body has many other consequences as well. When any irritating liquid is repeatedly injected into a vein, that vein becomes irritated or inflamed. If this condition persists, it progresses to blood vessel irritation or vasculitis. Addicts have also made the mistake of injecting cocaine into an artery rather than a vein. Arteries react to the irritation by constricting. This constriction decreases the amount of blood that flows through the artery. The decreased blood supply to the arm or leg (or any other area that the artery supplies) causes the tissue downstream to die. Addicts have lost fingers, arms, or legs due to the complications of injecting cocaine into an artery.

There are several other common complications of intravenous cocaine use. Recurrent injections in the frenzy produced by cocaine causes scarring of the skin at injection sites. Bacteria introduced at the injection site produce local abscesses. Injection of foreign matter (talc, bacteria, mold, or dust) contained in the cocaine solution can block the small capillaries in the lungs, decreasing lung function permanently.

Freebasing or crack smoking

Freebasing or crack smoking is associated with damage to the lungs through the continued inhalation of toxic cocaine vapors. Constriction of the vocal cords, constant hoarseness, and the effects of bronchitis persist long after one stops smoking cocaine. Bronchitis is an irritation, inflammation, or infection of the larger airway tubes of the lungs. Cocaine smoke first irritates the trachea and bronchi. These tubes then can not carry out their cleansing functions properly. This may lead to an infection in the lungs, bronchitis or pneumonia.

As cocaine passes by the delicate vocal cords, it irritates them as well. This irritation leads to constriction of the blood supply to the vocal cords. After short-term use, some cocaine smokers report voice problems for months. Cocaine vapors pass through the large airways entering the bronchioles. The vapors then enter the alveoli. The bronchioles are smaller tubes designed to carry air to the alveoli. The alveoli, as noted previously, are very small sacks that extract oxygen from the air to enter the bloodstream. Alveoli also discharge carbon dioxide from our bloodstream into the air. Cocaine irritates these delicate lung parts. As of the writing of this book, it is unclear whether cocaine smoking causes permanent lung damage to the bronchioles and alveoli of the lungs.

Another odd complication of cocaine smoking is air (pneumo-) in the space around the heart (mediastinum). Pneumomediastinum occurs when air escapes from the lungs into the space around the heart and its large blood vessels in the center of the chest. Cocaine addicts inhale cocaine deeply into the lungs and attempt to hold this air for some time by closing the mouth. The increased pressure on the lungs in combination with the irritation of cocaine on the lungs can force air out through a rent in the lungs. Frequently, the escaped air and cocaine vapors are pushed into the heart's protective space. The air pressure and cocaine vapors irritate the heart, causing rhythm disturbances. Deaths have been reported from cocaine vapor pneumomediastinum.

In addition, freebase or crack smoking is associated with fires. This happens when individuals manufacture the base form of cocaine by using volatile solvents such as ethyl ether or ethanol. The number of fire related accidents has led freebase smokers to use other solvents (most commonly water) to extract freebase cocaine or crack from the salt form of the cocaine.

However the drug is administered, there are frequent toxic side effects resulting from the ingestion of a very powerful drug into the body. We will discuss the complications of cocaine on each of the major organs of the body.

Effects on the heart and other muscles

The heart is very susceptible to the effects of cocaine. Small to moderate doses of cocaine accelerate the heart rate. Higher doses of cocaine bring about rhythm disturbances of the heart. Rhythm disturbances are the most common complication from the use of cocaine. The user may feel the rhythm disturbances as an acceleration of the pulse with mild chest discomfort, a fluttering sensation in the chest, or an interruption in the normal beating pattern of the heart (heart palpitations). The heart must maintain a consistent rhythm pattern to pump blood efficiently. Rhythm disturbances can result in heart standstill and death.

Large doses of cocaine decrease the heart's own blood supply, at times causing a heart attack (myocardial infarction). Heart attacks are often felt as a heavy pressure sensation on the chest with pain radiating down the arm. Heart attacks can occur, however, without pain or warning. Heart attacks destroy part of the heart muscle. Once heart muscle dies, it cannot be restored. If enough muscle is lost in a heart attack, the heart can no longer pump blood, and the heart attack victim dies. Cocaine users that have a strong family history of heart disease may be at greater risk for heart problems from the use of cocaine. Large doses of cocaine seem to damage the heart muscle directly and occasionally produce instant death.

Other muscles in the body are also affected by cocaine. Addicts who use cocaine frequently report pain in their calf muscles, their jaw muscles, or their backs. Cocaine is directly toxic to muscle tissue. When muscles are irritated, they break down muscle protein. Routine laboratory chemistry tests detect these proteins, and indicate the extent of acute muscle damage. Noncardiac (skeletal) muscle can be rebuilt by the body. The body's muscles are also irritated indirectly through stimulation of the muscle by the brain. As the brain becomes agitated with cocaine, it sends out signals to the muscles to contract. This sustained (tonic) contraction of the muscles seems to intensify muscle cramping during cocaine use. Moderate doses of cocaine also cause muscle twitching or tics which accompany cocaine toxicity.

Effects on the liver

The liver is responsible for metabolizing (breaking down) cocaine. When large doses of cocaine are consumed, the liver is unable to process all of the cocaine quickly. This slows down the rate of elimination of cocaine from the body. The overload of cocaine, especially when consumed with alcohol or other drugs, damages the liver. Alcohol, sedatives, and narcotics are all detoxified in the liver. When an addict combines cocaine with other drugs, the liver must detoxify a large quantity and diversity of chemicals. If the addict uses frequently, his liver is taxed beyond its ability to metabolize these drugs. The taxed liver is damaged by the repeated stress of exposure to too much alcohol and too many drugs. If during the course of drug use the addict is exposed to the hepatitis virus, the liver is *doubly damaged* by the combination of hepatitis virus inflammation and drug detoxification.

The liver indicates it is damaged by dropping some of its enzymes into the bloodstream. These enzymes are detected on routine blood chemistry tests. If liver damage occurs, the most effective treatment is proper diet, rest, and cocaine abstinence. Unless the cocaine addict has hepatitis, the damage by cocaine alone is often reversible. If the addict has consumed large quantities of alcohol, he runs the risk of cirrhosis, like any other alcoholic.

Effects on the brain

The brain is very sensitive to the toxic effects of cocaine. In this section, I will review cocaine's toxic effects on the physical brain. Cocaine actually creates the most damage in the thinking part of the brain, the mind. These effects are so diverse and intense, that the second half of this chapter (and Chapter Six) is dedicated to describing and overcoming the effects of cocaine on the mind.

The most frequent brain complication of cocaine use is seizures. Seizures created by cocaine are unrelated to the frequency or length of time that the drug is used, or the health of the individual. Seizures occur with low and high doses of cocaine. Fourteen percent of heavy cocaine users report having had at least one seizure. Crack and intravenous cocaine users have seizures more frequently. Cocaine seizures often go unnoticed by users that have them. Addicts will report their friends having seizures, but be unaware of their own seizures. They remain unaware of their own seizures because of retrograde amnesia; the seizure causes the victim to forget what happened around the time of the epileptic fit. Any cocaine user who has used alone may be unaware of his own seizures.

Cocaine-induced seizures are erratic and unpredictable. They have been reported in individuals who are first time users of cocaine. An individual who has used cocaine for many years may one day have his first cocaine seizure. After the brain has had one seizure, it may be trained to have more. In animal studies, when an animal has several cocaine-induced seizures, the repeated administration of cocaine over weeks or months trains the animal's brain to be susceptible to additional seizure activity. This process, known as *kindling*, creates a permanent change; once kindled by cocaine seizures, the brain remains more likely to have repeated seizures with or without additional cocaine. Kindling may also be related to cocaine cravings. Recent clinical research has shown that one antiseizure medication, carbamazepine (Tegretol®), reduces drug cravings. Researchers have postulated that cravings are small kindled localized seizures. Using this hypothesis, an antiseizure medication should reduce craving behaviors. See Chapter Four for more information.

Cocaine seizures can lead to cardiac standstill (a period during which the heart ceases to beat). Many cocaine deaths are instigated by a seizure during acute intoxication. The seizure causes heart rhythm problems. The heart rhythm problems, in turn, induce poor heart pumping action and the user dies.

Cocaine also affects the lower centers of the brain. The body's thermostat is located at the base of the brain. All using addicts have modifications in their thermostat functioning. With moderate doses of cocaine, the body turns up its thermostat. The muscles contract more frequently, thus increasing body temperature. The user sweats to combat the temperature increase. Large doses of cocaine may cause permanent damage from the direct effects of increased body temperature.

The breathing center is also at the base of the brain. This center is responsible for the regulation of the rate and rhythm of our breathing. With very high doses of cocaine the breathing center malfunctions, creating irregular breathing or a complete interruption in respiratory function. If this occurs for a prolonged period, the user dies.

Effects on the Mind

Cocaine is used for its effects on the mind—the thinking and feeling brain. The cocaine user snorts, shoots, or smokes cocaine to affect his thoughts and feelings. It seems ironic that the greatest damage occurs to the same mind that the user hoped to improve with cocaine. The acute effects of cocaine on our minds are well known. Euphoria, racing thoughts, reward, and feelings of well-being result from the short-term use of cocaine. However, the mind is left with depression, slowed thoughts, no motivation, and a life that seems to have no rewards other than cocaine. These toxic effects on the mind far outrank and outlast the short-term effects of cocaine.

Principle 3 — Of all the organs in the body, cocaine is most toxic to the brain.

Cocaine creates a sense of well-being when first used. This sense of well-being is called euphoria. Euphoria is followed by desires to consume more cocaine. This process is called reinforced-use craving, which is discussed in Chapter Five.

Reinforced-use craving drives the addict to perform extraordinary feats to obtain more cocaine. Reinforced-use craving is a biologic process seen in laboratory experiments with monkeys as well as in man.

Cocaine causes thinking to accelerate. The body feels tremulous and the mind becomes agitated. The cocaine addict soon shifts from a sense of well-being to an acute dysphoric state (dysphoric is the opposite of euphoric). Thinking becomes cloudy and users become suspicious. Often chronic cocaine users switch from using with friends to using in isolation, because they become paranoid of others. Often the paranoia is directed at authority figures. Adults believe the police are outside and adolescents hear their parents or school authorities. Auditory hallucinations (usually hearing whispers) are common during cocaine intoxication. The user's vision may be filled with small spots of light similar in type and cause to those seen during migraine headaches.

As the cocaine user develops a higher blood level of the drug, he appears to be unable to sense the euphoriant effect of cocaine. This inability to feel the effects of cocaine with repeated dosing is called *tolerance*. The mind develops tolerance to the effects of cocaine quickly. The body, however, *never* adjusts to the toxic effects of cocaine. The user consumes more and more cocaine to obtain the same effect. Since the body cannot adjust to this, it soon gives out. The mind's tolerance to the effects of cocaine frequently leads to inadvertent overdose. The addict feels less and less high from the drug and begins using more and more cocaine until he has a seizure, cardiac standstill, or respiratory collapse, and dies.

Although cocaine use has been attached to sexual activity in our folklore, the truth is far different. Cocaine addicts liken the initial use of cocaine, especially by the intravenous or smoking method, to sexual orgasm. When addicted, the cocaine user reports preferring cocaine to sex at least fifty percent of the time. The cocaine user who combines cocaine and sex may experience an initial increase in sexual performance, but continued cocaine use more frequently leads to difficulties with intercourse. The increased difficulties are combined with continued fantasies of sexual prowess. This leads the addict to compulsive and often bizarre sexual behaviors. After engaging in his sexual compulsions, the addict is left with shame and guilt. Once in recovery, the addict must externalize, experience, and resolve his shame about the past to fully recover. Sexual shame is best addressed in individual or group therapy. I will examine this further in Chapter Ten.

The final set of complications that arise from cocaine use are suicide and homicide. Cocaine addicts become very agitated and paranoid during a cocaine binge. On occasion, they hear voices or sounds that confirm their suspicions. If they are dealing the drug, they may have guns or other weapons at their disposal. During Stage I and II of the Cocaine Addiction Cycle (see Chapter Three), this paranoid state causes impulsive actions with weapons that result in gunshot and knife wounds or homicide.

Cocaine use causes extreme remorse and acute depression in Stage III of the Cocaine Addiction Cycle. During the cocaine crash, the addict may feel devastated, trapped, and simultaneously agitated. This cocaine crash drives many to suicide attempts or suicide. Addicts may intentionally overdose on cocaine or take their lives in other ways. Suicide is an unpredictable, acute response to the cocaine crash.

Principle 4 — Each one of us is unique; however, cocaine addiction reduces us to cocaine-using animals.

Cocaine had a reputation in the 1960s of being a safe, nonaddicting drug. This reputation has changed more recently, mostly as a result of the number of individuals who have become cocaine dependent in our society. The earlier reputation for being safe often remains planted in the minds of the using addict. He writes off recent news coverage as sensationalistic. Animal research, however, bypasses the societal effects and the sensationalistic news coverage. Animal research points to the most basic characteristics of cocaine addiction and underscores the destructive and compulsive qualities of cocaine addiction.

Monkey research has offered remarkable information about how cocaine affects the brain. The most direct information about the addiction potential of cocaine comes from a simple experimental design.

Rhesus monkeys, rats, cats, and baboons are placed in a cage with an intravenous catheter in one of their veins. The catheter runs from a bottle of cocaine solution. The flow of the solution is controlled by a pump, which is in turn programmed to deliver the drug to the animal depending upon which lever the animal chooses. The conditions under which the animal will administer the drug demonstrate the biologic qualities of the addictive use of any given drug.

Such studies allow researchers to discuss cocaine addiction without the bias of human studies. That is, researchers will not attribute the compulsive use of cocaine to either the poor relationship of a given rat with its mother or the socioeconomic deprivation of a particular species of monkey. Upbringing and socioeconomic factors do have a part in addictions. Animal models, however, define the animal portion of man's nature. Animal experimentation tells us that:

- Rhesus monkeys, when given a choice between cocaine and food, will continue to choose cocaine until they are severely debilitated.
- Monkeys, given the choice between cocaine and the chance to socialize with another monkey, will choose cocaine exclusively.
- Monkeys, when sex deprived, choose cocaine over sex.
- Monkeys will administer cocaine to themselves despite knowing that following the drug administration they will receive a painful electrical shock.
- All animals, given free access to cocaine, will self-administer the drug in bursts mimicking the binging behavior seen in humans. Some animals will administer the drug to the point of death.

We are not monkeys. Each one of us is unique. We are unique in many ways—how we think, what we enjoy in life, and how we go about solving tasks and problems. We are also human beings, primates, the animal *Homo sapiens*. Given a chance to learn and grow without inhibitions, we become animals with a marvelous variety of thoughts and dreams. We build bridges, adapt to change, and exercise curiosity about the world around us.

When exposed to cocaine, however, the animal *Homo sapiens* becomes a self-destructive beast obsessed with using cocaine, choosing the drug over food, sex, and socializing. We use despite the painful consequences of our drug use. The variety of thoughts and experiences we characterize as human falls by the wayside. We exhibit the same stereotypical patterns of cocaine usage as the lower primates.

When addicted, man will prefer using cocaine to almost all other activities. He will continue to use until he runs out of drugs or money or becomes physically exhausted. Man has shown how like the monkey he is when given free access to cocaine. Cocaine addicts report preferring cocaine to sex or food when hungry. Man will use cocaine despite the adverse consequences of drug toxicity and the common consequences of chest pain, heart attack, and seizures. Given free access to large quantities of the drug, man—the animal—often overdoses and dies. Animal studies imply that cocaine is such a powerful reinforcer of its own use that, given sufficient access, almost anyone can become addicted.

Cocaine use causes many, more subtle changes in our behaviors. As human beings, we relish feeling in control of our lives. We feel more secure if we are able to make sense out of our behavior. Our minds continuously analyze our actions. However, this rational mind of which we are so proud has no ability to comprehend the power of cocaine. Cocaine bypasses the rational part of our mind, acting directly on the brain's reward center. Once the user has the first hit, cocaine creates a need or drive to consume more.

Cocaine induces a sense of reward by stimulating a small area in the medial prefrontal cortex. This area of the brain is responsible for the appreciation of all rewards. Cocaine triggers a reward response that is indistinguishable from the reward of a fine meal, falling in love, being given a present, or receiving a bonus at work.

All rewards involve change. A change from being hungry to being satiated, thirsty to quenched, financially troubled to financially secure. The edge of the reward (moving from the unrewarded to rewarded state) creates euphoria. Our minds quickly habituate or develop tolerance to any reward. For example, if one is out of work for a time and has financial troubles, the first paycheck seems like a million dollars. When the work is steady, paychecks come every two weeks and the financial crisis is over—payday seems more of a given and less of a reward. The euphoria created by the change to financial stability is replaced by everyday life. The mind shifts to other goals in life in order to feel reward.

Cocaine drives the reward mechanism and floods it mercilessly. Conventional goals lose their meaning. The addict drifts away from work, relationships, and from developing leisure activities when he is using cocaine. He has found a direct biochemical substitute for all his needs. All of us strive in life for those things we find meaningful. To a large extent, this search for meaning is driven by the animal part of us that feels reward for accomplishing a task. When a person uses cocaine, he finds a task that indeed seems meaningful. After all, it brings on a large reward! This mechanism fosters the development of convoluted behaviors that a user establishes to continue his cocaine habit.

A problem arises because cocaine fires the reward center directly, without any of the usual behaviors that the mind recognizes as reward producing. Cocaine becomes very important, but the mind cannot understand why. In order for the addict to continue in the pursuit of cocaine, he develops elaborate rationalizations for his behavior. When one looks at the money, time, health, and relationships lost to cocaine, it does not make sense to the rational mind. The conflict between the primitive drive and the rational self creates the psychological mechanism of denial. The rational mind looks at how much money is spent on cocaine and it does not compute. In order for it to make sense, the addict develops a series of theories, such as, "My spouse would just spend it on something silly anyway!" or "As hard as I work I deserve to spend ninety percent of my income on cocaine!" Unless an addict is able to see past his denial, he will return to cocaine use. These rationalizations, excuses, and beliefs about cocaine will continue to endanger the recovering mind, leading the unsuspecting addict to relapse.

I have described some of the ways that cocaine affects the mind. Some are obvious, such as depression that leads to suicide; and some are subtle, such as how our reward system is short-circuited to believe that the only meaningful reward in life is cocaine. In Chapter Six I will examine further how cocaine affects the mind in recovery, and how to retrain the mind to avoid cocaine-obsessed thinking patterns.

THREE

The Cocaine Addiction Cycle

Principles

1. Once addicted, the cocaine user falls into a cyclic use pattern.

2. The Cocaine Addiction Cycle is divided into five distinct stages.

3. The addict can recover, but only when he pulls himself completely out of the Cocaine Addiction Cycle.

This chapter will describe the repeatable patterns that cocaine users develop as they progress into cocaine addiction. These patterns are created by the toxic effects of cocaine on the brain. Much like the monkey described in Chapter Two, the cocaine user becomes trained in destructive patterns. These patterns evolve without the user's conscious knowledge. Cocaine cannot be used continuously. Instead, the vast majority of cocaine users are entrained by cocaine to alternate between periods of compulsive consumption and complete abstinence. This is the Cocaine Addiction Cycle.

Most cocaine addicts begin using cocaine casually on the weekends or at social functions. Use may be sporadic for a period of time, especially if one begins using the drug by insufflation (snorting). If a user continues to snort the drug, his binge pattern becomes more and more regular. He may start using every weekend, or every payday. He may escalate rapidly, until he snorts the drug each evening. Most addicts engage in the addiction cycle by establishing a characteristic pattern, alternating between use and forced abstinence. As the snorting episodes intensify, the user develops increasingly bizarre cocaine rituals.

Some people begin their addiction by smoking or shooting cocaine from the start. Friends commonly introduce others to smoking or shooting cocaine. If this happens, and one is susceptible[1] to the effects of cocaine, the addiction may take hold immediately. One or two episodes of smoking crack or injecting cocaine can lead to compulsive binges that continue until the money or thecocaine is gone.

Principle 1 — Once addicted, the cocaine user falls into a cyclic use pattern.

A cocaine user may be unaware at first of how his use of cocaine has changed. A casual user may find himself thinking, "It isn't a party without a little coke!" or "It's a long weekend, time for cocaine!" Initial casual use has, at this point, shifted into heavier use with less control over the amount used and the amount of time spent using. The binges become more periodic, and more frequent vows to never use again are made during the post-cocaine crash. The addict may find that he makes a commitment on Monday not to use that coming week. By Friday, the user holds his paycheck in his hand as he drives to the dealer's house. He is compelled by the Cocaine Addiction Cycle to use again.

---

1. Almost all researchers in the field of addiction agree that certain individuals seem more prone to develop addiction than others. This tendency may be determined by genetic factors, an individual's sociological pressures, or by the components of one's internal psychological structure. Increasing evidence points to a genetic (inherited) tendency to develop alcoholism. Many clinicians assert that all addictive diseases have a strong genetic component, based on evidence from alcoholism research. The works of Wallace and Goodwin (see *Additional Readings* at the end of Part One) discuss the genetic and biologic characteristics of addiction. Other researchers indicate that cocaine addiction occurs in psychologically susceptible individuals, as in the works of Khantzian and Gawin (see *Additional Readings*). Sociologists point out that dispossessed segments of society have a high incidence of addictive diseases (e.g. American Indians and the Alaskan Eskimo) and therefore point to societal problems in the genesis of addictive disease.

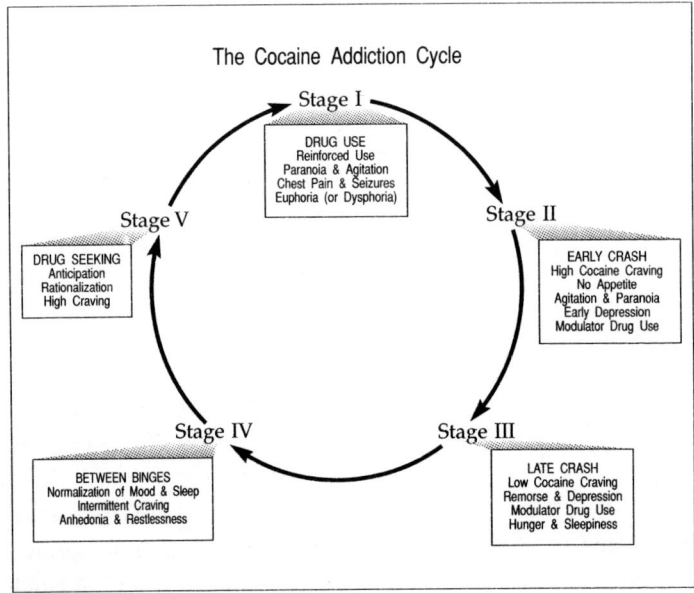

Figure 3
When an addict becomes addicted to cocaine, he begins using in a cyclic pattern known as the Cocaine Addiction Cycle. To recover, the addict must be completely removed from this cycle.

What makes up the addiction cycle? This will be examined in some depth. The exercises in *The Cocaine Recovery Workbook* will help an addict understand his own pattern of use. Once an addict is clear about the addiction cycle, he will know how to extract himself from that cycle with the help of treatment and the tools described in Part Two of this book.

Principle 2 — The Cocaine Addiction Cycle is divided into five distinct stages.

Cocaine consumption only occurs in Stage I of the Cocaine Addiction Cycle. Once an addict stops the binge consumption of the drug, he moves to Stage II. The crash from the cocaine high occurs in two distinct phases: Stages II and III. The addict most often ends Stage III with a long sleep. Awaking the next morning with little drug craving, the addict pronounces himself cured. This is Stage IV in the addiction cycle. Stage IV is the most variable in length. People who are in Stage IV emphatically state: "I'll never use cocaine again." The addict then moves from Stage IV to Stage V. This movement is triggered by various cues that ignite cocaine craving. If an addict rationalizes using cocaine again and begins searching for the drug, he is in Stage V. If, in turn, he is successful in obtaining cocaine, he returns to Stage I, the using stage. The Cocaine Addiction Cycle is illustrated in Figure 3. Let us examine each stage in more detail.

STAGE I - Cocaine Consumption

Stage I may start innocently enough. If a cocaine user is early in his addiction, he may just use a small quantity of cocaine at a bar or with friends. It makes him feel good. He decides to use more and sets out to find additional cocaine.

As the user progresses into addiction, he may need to rationalize his cocaine use. Remembering his last cocaine episode, he tells himself that he will only consume a small quantity of cocaine this time. Toward this end, he may purchase a small quantity, telling himself, "This time I will have a little better control and buy only a small amount." As soon as this amount is consumed, he experiences almost immediate cravings for more. These cravings produce the continued obsessive use characteristic of each binge.

An addict late in the progression of cocaine addiction may find that many of the rationalizations about cocaine use have completely dropped away. He is driven to consume large quantities at great expense and spend long hours binging on cocaine. He knows he is an addict and knows that he is out of control. At this point, however, he doesn't care. He will purchase a large quantity of the drug, knowing all too well that he will go into a full blown cocaine binge.

However Stage I begins, once an addict starts, the rest of the binge follows a predictable course. When the initial euphoric effect of the drug begins to wear off, the addict experiences almost immediate cravings for more cocaine. These cravings are very intense, coming from outside of the addict's own rational self. The addict rationalizes the continued use of the drug saying, "This cocaine was not strong enough" or "It would have worked, if I had bought enough in the first place." While in this phase of the binge, the addict will find himself returning immediately to the source of the drug to purchase more. If he has ready access to the drug or already has a large quantity on hand, he will compulsively use more and more—unable to stop.

After repeated use, cocaine does not create any appreciable euphoria. In fact, the addict may feel somewhat despondent and dysphoric. He finds that each subsequent dose seems to do less toward making him feel good, despite increasing the dose. The lack of euphoria does nothing to stop the cravings.

Later in the binge, the addict finds himself very intoxicated and beginning to experience many of the side effects of cocaine. He may see small flicks of light flashing in front of his vision (cocaine lights). He experiences paranoia. If he began using with others, he leaves these friends so he can use alone in peace. He becomes suspicious of those around him or wonders if the police or some other authority figure know about his cocaine use. His pulse begins to race and his chest begins to ache. It is often during this phase that the addict regrets using cocaine in the first place. If more cocaine is available, the overpowering drive to use more usually overwhelms this feeling of remorse. The addict is left searching for more money and more cocaine. This continues until no more cocaine is to be had.

Cocaine addicts find the physical interruption of the drug supply (such as a dealer who has gone away or to bed), the lack of money, or their own physical exhaustion to be the sole factors in discontinuing their cocaine binges. Often, the cocaine addict binges long into the night or next day, missing work, or showing up late for appointments. It is in the midst of such a binge that seizures occur. The cocaine user may also feel chest pain; many develop the symptoms of heart attack and heart standstill. Despite the fact that the drug level remains very high in the body, each repeated dose of cocaine seems less effective. This disparity between the increasing toxic effects of cocaine and the decreasing euphoric effect pushes the cocaine addict to consume huge quantities, sometimes resulting in life-threatening overdoses.

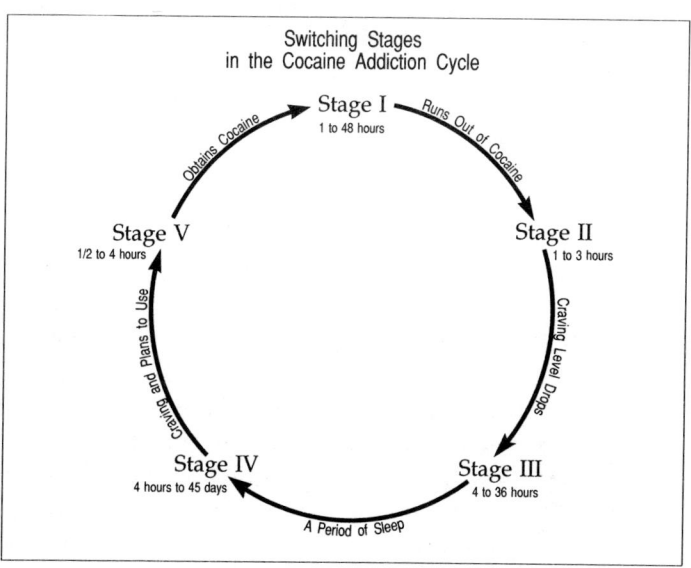

Figure 4
Specific events move the addict from stage to stage in the Cocaine Addiction Cycle.

Late in the binge, cocaine addicts often find themselves pacing around the house, or consuming other drugs to modulate the effects of cocaine on the body. Addicts may consume alcohol, sedative drugs such as diazepam (Valium®), chlordiazepoxide (Librium®), lorazepam (Ativan®), alprazolam (Xanax®), and flurazepam (Dalmane®), barbiturates, or narcotics to temper the effects of cocaine on the body. Addicts use modulator drugs to temper cocaine's undesirable side effects on the mind as well. Late in Stage I, an addict may find himself craving the modulator drugs and may consume them in large quantities.

When the addict runs out of money or cocaine or the dealer is no longer available, the drug binge ends. Cocaine dealers or other individuals who have access to huge quantities of the drug find themselves discontinuing their cocaine binge only because they are too exhausted to manage administering more cocaine.

STAGE II - Early Crash
Stage II begins at the end of the actual binge of cocaine consumption. Stage II is typified by intense feelings of anxiety. Drug craving remains extremely high and the addict finds himself searching for ways of obtaining more money or more cocaine. Often, despite his full rational knowledge that there is no way that more cocaine can be obtained, the addict develops fantasies about more drugs being available. Cocaine addicts will search the floor for small white flecks of dust or lint that resemble cocaine. They may think about a small stash they have hidden somewhere despite their rational mind knowing that the stash was consumed weeks ago. The hyperactivity that started in Stage I continues—they pace the floor.

Despite being used in large quantities, the modulator drugs do little to temper the effects of cocaine on the mind. Cocaine users who rarely drink unless on a cocaine binge, find themselves consuming large amounts of alcohol in Stage II. Addicts swallow handfuls of sedatives, huge quantities of marijuana or narcotics to cut the edge off the cocaine crash.

During Stage II, the addict's hunger for food is extremely low. Often the idea of food is revolting. His body temperature is very high and, as a result, he sweats profusely. Due to time distortion, Stage II appears to last a long time. Several hours of intense cocaine craving feels like several days. In fact, this stage of the cocaine crash lasts about one to four hours, depending on the amount of the drug consumed. In Stage II, the addict begins to feel remorse about this binge. The onset of remorse marks the transition into Stage III.

STAGE III - Late Crash
Stage III begins when, over the course of one-half hour, the drug craving shifts from a very high level to a very low level. Stage III usually begins within three to five hours of the last cocaine use. In Stage III, the addict feels extremely depressed and remorseful but, at the same time, less anxious. He begins to feel hungry and, at times, he either feels sleepy or dazed. Later in Stage III, the addict begins to doze. If he remains awake, he is hungry and often eats voraciously.

It is in Stage III that addicts feel the most intense remorse over what they have done. In fact, all the shame and self-deprecatory thoughts from the entire addiction cycle are magnified in Stage III. This remorse propels addicts to consider suicide, running away, or entering treatment. The majority of emergency calls to treatment centers and drug hot lines occur in Stage III. In this stage, the agitation seems to subside. Because the agitation is less, the addict discontinues his consumption of modulator drugs. Stage III is filled with ultimatums, such as: "I'll never do this again!" and "If you get me through this one, God, I'll never be tempted again." Any ultimatum or pledge seems sincere, well meaning, and lasting. As well intentioned as these ultimatums appear, the addict moves on to minimize his addiction dilemma in Stage IV.

STAGE IV - Between Binges

The addict, twenty-four to forty-eight hours after his last cocaine binge, experiences an improving mood and outlook on life. He senses relief, having made it through the horror of the binge. He may have feelings of uniqueness or grandiosity about his ability to cope with cocaine. His friends have had social and medical problems from their cocaine usage, but he believes it will never happen to him! Unfortunately, this grandiosity can only lead the addict to relapse.

During Stage IV, the addict believes his mood is returning to normal. His sleep patterns normalize. He may experience an increasing amount of energy, but at times he feels restless. This is combined with a deeper feeling of emptiness. The cocaine has flooded and shorted out the natural reward mechanisms, making life seem without meaning or goals. This flat, grey feeling is called anhedonia. Anhedonia is characteristic of addicts in Stage IV.

After surviving each cocaine binge and living through the post-cocaine crash, the addict usually feels he has overcome his cocaine problem. Despite the fact that he used four or five days ago, he believes he has his drug problem under control. He believes he has lived up to all the grand ultimatums made in Stage III; after all, he has stopped using for the past four days! During Stage IV, the addict feels that cocaine has little, if any, power over his mind. In truth, the toxic effects of cocaine remain intense; they have simply gone underground into his subconscious.

In Stage IV, the addict will experience drug craving episodes. Craving is often triggered by exposure to cocaine, spending time with cocaine-using friends, or having available cash. If the addict encourages the drug craving for a period of time, he will proceed into Stage V, the drug seeking stage. This will start the cycle all over again. On the other hand, the addict may spend an extended amount of time in Stage IV and not recover from cocaine dependence. Without treatment, addicts are unable to disentangle themselves from the addiction cycle, and suffer a forced abstinence. The addict may remain in Stage IV for long periods of time, experience a seemingly normal mood without sleep problems, and have intermittent cravings for the drug. This is the most insidious and troublesome part of the Cocaine Addiction Cycle. If the addict does not seek treatment, he will endure long periods of emptiness and discontent.

Stage IV does offer hope. It is out of Stage IV that the recovery reflex begins. The recovery reflex is a natural response to the trauma of being chemically dependent; a response that occurs when an addict discontinues addicting chemicals. The tools for this reflex are fully described in Part Two of this book. Stage IV is, then, a fork in the road. One half of the fork leads to recovery; the other to Stage V and continued use. Part Two of this book describes how the addict extracts himself from the Cocaine Addiction Cycle and moves into recovery.

STAGE V - Drug Seeking

In Stage V, the addict finds himself flipping from the cured feeling of Stage IV to the drug craving characteristic of Stage V. Because he is deluded into believing his cocaine problem is under control, the addict frequently makes foolhardy decisions while in Stage IV. He may feel he can handle being around friends who are using. Or he may return to selling cocaine to make up for the large amount of money he spent on drugs. If the addict is able to resist using after being exposed to cocaine, he develops a false sense of security. Repeated exposure to the drug eventually causes an intense craving, and the addiction cycle continues.

Other environmental or internal cues trigger craving as well. Craving can be brought on by music, thoughts about using (good or bad), or simply discussing a past binge with a friend. Craving can also be triggered by certain locations, a racing heart, or even gastrointestinal distress.

Once the addict begins craving and decides that he needs cocaine, the drug seeking of Stage V begins. The cocaine-seeking behavior of Stage V is persistent and driving. Addicts who are impatient about everything else will wait hours for their dealer's phone call. Late in addiction, drug seeking has a panicky quality. Thus, the cocaine addict will wake up friends in the middle of the night seeking the drug or drive long distances to obtain cocaine. The addict experiences tremendous anticipation about the effects of the drug. The anticipation only serves to augment the drug seeking in a vicious circle.

This anticipation is called the *pre-cocaine jitters*. These jitters consist of a dry mouth, a racing pulse, cold sweaty palms, and hypermotility of the gastrointestinal tract. This experience is similar to being very anxious prior to a speech or other performance. The euphoric qualities of past cocaine highs add a strong edge of anticipation to the jittery pre-cocaine feeling.

Stage V is filled with rationalizations. The addict may tell himself that he will only use a small amount or stop himself before he becomes out of control. These rationalizations arise despite the fact that after each previous time the addict used cocaine, he found himself in deep trouble. Rationalizations diminish the true impact of cocaine dependence on the addict, and allow the drug seeking behavior to continue.

If the addict is successful in obtaining cocaine, Stage I recurs and the Cocaine Addiction Cycle continues.

Principle 3 — The addict can recover, but only when he pulls himself completely out of the Cocaine Addiction Cycle.

When a person becomes entangled in the Cocaine Addiction Cycle, he shifts from a unique individual to an individual who is constantly using, recovering from the crash, attempting to normalize his thoughts about the using world, and then finding ways and means of getting more cocaine. This results in more cocaine use, and another turn around the Cocaine Addiction Cycle. The cycle can be completed once a month or once a day. Once entrenched in the cocaine addiction cycle, the cycle itself becomes a learned pattern for living—a repeatable, endless loop in the brain. Addicts enter treatment late in Stage III or in Stage IV. While in treatment, the addict has the opportunity to completely remove himself from the addiction cycle.

Not all cocaine users consume cocaine in the addiction cycle described in this chapter. If a person does not use in a cyclic pattern, it may indicate that he has biochemical differences from other cocaine addicts. If an addict believes that his use of cocaine is different, he should discuss this with a therapist or doctor.

Recovery is not about training oneself not to use. Recovery is a shift or transformation completely out of the Cocaine Addiction Cycle. This transformation does not delay or repress the Cocaine Addiction Cycle. Instead, recovery pulls the addict out of the cycle altogether. Once out of the cycle, the possibility of a life with enriching growth is opened up. In Part Two, I will describe the process of recovery. Cocaine quickly trains the mind in self-destructive patterns. Deprogramming the mind from the effects of cocaine is more difficult. Part Two contains techniques to assist the recovery reflex, permanently removing the addict from the Cocaine Addiction Cycle.

Additional Readings for Part One

Acquired Immunodeficiency Syndrome and Chemical Dependency. Washington, DC: *NIAAA Publication*, 88-1513, 1987.

Alcoholics Anonymous, third edition. New York, NY: Alcoholics Anonymous World Services, 1976.

Berenson, D. "Alcoholics Anonymous: From Surrender to Transformation." *The Family Therapy Networker*, Vol. 11(4): 25-31, 1987.

Byck, R. (Ed.) *Cocaine Papers: Sigmund Freud.* New York, NY: Stonehill, 1974.

Fischman, M. W. "Behavioral Pharmacology of Cocaine." *Journal of Clinical Psychiatry*, 49[2,Suppl]:7-10, 1988.

Gawin, F. H., & H. D. Kleber. "Abstinence Symptomatology and Psychiatric Diagnosis in Cocaine Abusers." *Archives of General Psychiatry*, 43:107-113, 1986.

Gazzaniga, M. *The Social Brain: Discovering the Networks of the Mind.* New York, NY: Basic Books, 1969.

Gold, M. S., & A. M. Washton. "Adverse Effects on Health and Function of Cocaine Abuse: Data from 800-Cocaine Callers." *NIDA Monograph*, 1(2):18, 1984.

Gong, V., & N. Rudnick. (Eds.) *AIDS: Facts and Issues.* New Brunswick, NJ: Rutgers University Press, 1986.

Goodwin, D. W. "Genetic Influences in Alcoholism." *Advances in Internal Medicine*, 32:283-97, 1987.

Goodwin, D. W. "Genetic Factors in the Development of Alcoholism." *Psychiatric Clinics of North America*, Sept:9(3):427-33, 1986.

Khantzian, E. J. "The Self-medication Hypothesis of Addictive Disorders: Focus on Heroin and Cocaine Dependence." *American Journal of Psychiatry*, Nov:142(11):1259-64, 1974.

Kleber H. D. "Introduction: Cocaine Abuse: Historical, Epidemiological, and Psychological Perspectives." *Journal of Clinical Psychiatry*, 49 (Suppl):3-7, 1989.

Nahas, G. *Cocaine: The Great White Plague.* Middlebury, VT: Eriksson, 1989.

Narcotics Anonymous. C.A.R.E.N.A. Publishing, 1982.

Twelve Steps and Twelve Traditions. New York, NY: Alcoholics Anonymous World Services, 1981.

Wallace, J. *Alcoholism: New Light on the Disease.* Newport, RI: Edgehill Publications, 1987.

Washton, A. M., M. S. Gold, & A. L. Pottash. "Survey of 500 Callers to a National Cocaine Help Line." *Psychosomatics*, 25:10-15, 1984.

PART TWO

The Recovery Reflex

Introductory Remarks

Principles

1. A cocaine addict needs to assess his commitment to recovery and a drug-free lifestyle on a daily basis.

2. The recovery reflex is a natural reflex of the mind. It occurs when each of the following happens to the addicted brain:
   - The brain is freed from all mind-altering chemicals and their long-term toxic effects.
   - The most intense conflicts of the past are addressed and at least partially resolved.
   - The mind is exposed to order and direction, usually by means of a spiritual experience.

In Part Two, I will address the process of recovery from cocaine dependence. The recovery process from cocaine addiction is similar to recovery from other addictive chemicals or behaviors. Addiction recovery is a natural reflex of the mind that occurs if a series of specific obstacles are removed from the addict's path. The most successful and rewarding path of recovery is through the Twelve Steps, as first used for alcohol dependence. This book discusses briefly the twelve-step path of recovery in Chapter Eight. The first four chapters of Part Two may be seen as a compendium of the obstacles in the path to recovery. The obstacles are:
   - Cocaine detoxification and toxicity (Chapter Four)
   - Cocaine craving (Chapter Five)
   - Cognitive (thinking) problems (Chapter Six)
   - Mood problems early in recovery (Chapter Seven).

In treatment, patients are exposed to twelve-step recovery from the day they enter a program. Twelve-step recovery is best taught through exposure to twelve-step meetings and people in recovery. It is never learned from a book. I have purposely avoided a deep discussion of the meaning of twelve-step recovery, lest anyone think that reading my discussion will replace an active struggle with the steps themselves. Thus, the discussion of the Twelve Steps appears near the end of this book. Once twelve-step recovery has begun, the addict should focus on preventing relapse. Chapter Nine describes a comprehensive relapse-prevention program for cocaine addicts. Part Two concludes with a discussion of some of the long-term therapy issues in cocaine recovery.

After reading the first part of this book, one should comprehend several key consequences that have accumulated in the migration from casual cocaine use to cocaine addiction. First, an addict begins chasing the elusive experience he felt from his first cocaine high. Second, the cocaine use becomes entrenched in the Cocaine Addiction Cycle. Third, his cocaine use restricts his life experiences. And finally the mind becomes toxic from the long-term effects of cocaine and other drug abuse. The drug user is caught in addiction, a process that blinds the addict from seeing its presence. The very thing that entraps the addict prevents him from seeing or believing that the trap even exists.

The reader may be saying, "Yes, I know that I am (or my loved one is) caught in this cycle, but how do I (or they) get out?" The remainder of this book contains techniques which, when used in conjunction with treatment, lead the addict out of the Cocaine Addiction Cycle.

Principle 1 — A cocaine addict needs to assess his commitment to recovery and a drug-free lifestyle on a daily basis.

The first goal in recovery from cocaine dependence is to be physically present in a recovery program or other treatment. A recovery program may entail outpatient or inpatient treatment, living in a recovery residence, individual or group psychotherapy, attendance at twelve-step recovery meetings or other support groups, and educational lectures. All of these components are part of the initial treatment of cocaine dependence. Being there, at first, means having one's body

Introductory Remarks

physically present. Being there during the first day or so is all that is necessary. I often tell patients that they need to bring their bodies first; their minds and their thoughts will arrive later.

Most addicts enter a hospital or treatment program during Stage II or III of the Cocaine Addiction Cycle. An addict may feel one of several ways about being in treatment:

1. "Yes, I have a cocaine problem. I use frequently and would like to use less often, maybe just on the weekends." Or perhaps, "I freebase cocaine and would sure like to return to snorting it."

2. "Yes, I use cocaine, I am in trouble, and I would like to stop using it—at least for several weeks, to get my life straightened out."

3. "Yes, I have a cocaine problem—it is way out of control. Otherwise, my life seems just fine. I don't want to change anything else."

4. "Yes, I have a cocaine problem—it is quite overwhelming. I want to stop cocaine. I have other problems in my life as well and would sure like to have them fixed while I'm in treatment. However, I don't want to stop using alcohol, marijuana, or other drugs."

5. "Yes, I have a cocaine problem and it is quite devastating. In addition, I have become addicted to alcohol and other drugs. I can't think of quitting for the rest of my life, but I am here to try this out."

6. "Yes, I have a cocaine problem and I want to quit cocaine and whatever else you say I must. My life is a mess; I will do just about anything."

If the reader is an addict in treatment, it may be helpful for him to take a moment for honest self-reflection and place himself in one of these categories. Addicts gain nothing by refusing to look at the reality of what has happened to their lives due to their drug addiction. If the reader is using *The Cocaine Recovery Workbook*, he should begin working the Daily Self-Assessment now. The Daily Self-Assessment is at the back of the workbook.

It is *not* important in early treatment to profess a firm commitment to stopping cocaine forever. Many people do not want to stop cocaine forever until they have been away from it for months or even years. Other people have periods of strong commitment to recovery followed by periods of doubt. This vacillation in commitment is normal. Most recovering addicts find that when they are having frequent cocaine craving episodes they feel less committed to recovery.

Remember, early in treatment an addict is still toxic from the effects of cocaine. Cocaine toxicity clouds the thinking and keeps one from seeing that the problem is as large as it is. When I confront patients regarding the level of their distorted thinking when coming off cocaine, they seem blinded by this distortion. This is one of the subtle and insidious complications of cocaine dependence. More often than not, this distortion causes patients to sabotage treatment; they believe that they are in better shape than they are.

The information presented in Part Two is just that, information. Understanding cocaine addiction does not make one drug-free. When an addict understands the problems of being cocaine dependent he can begin to recover. He must permit his attitudes and feelings about life to change. Change is the real work of recovery!

Principle 2 — The recovery reflex is a natural reflex of the mind. It occurs when each of the following happens to the addicted brain:
- The brain is freed from all mind-altering chemicals and their long-term toxic effects.
- The most intense conflicts of the past are addressed and at least partially resolved.
- The mind is exposed to order and direction, usually by means of a spiritual experience.

A reflex is a movement that occurs in response to a stimulus. Addicts use drugs expecting to feel good or have their lives changed in happy ways. Instead, they are traumatized by their compulsive drug use. Using addicts rarely see how they are traumatized by their addiction. Once recognized in early recovery, however, the trauma of addiction becomes the stimulus for the recovery reflex. When an addict's mind is freed from drugs, it begins to react, to search for meaning. This reactive search for meaning is the recovery reflex.

Every addict who recovers from a binge begins the recovery reflex when he asks, "Why did I do that again?" However, drug craving and recurrent drug use suppress any additional searching. Thus, the reflex is fragile, and needs to be guided by a recovery program.

A recovery program should contain three elements that insure the continuation of the recovery reflex. The first element involves freeing the mind from the confinement of alcohol and drug use. This usually occurs in an inpatient treatment setting. The second element involves facing the conflicts of the past. These conflicts may have only started with cocaine use. It is more likely, however, that pain, grief, loss, physical or sexual abuse, and resentment began before the user consumed addicting chemicals. In treatment, addicts are reintroduced to their problems. Some of the conflicts are addressed and resolved. Others are simply identified and placed on a *to do* list. Conflicts about the past that are not resolved during formal treatment are left for resolution in post-treatment twelve-step groups or in psychotherapy.

The third element begins, in a small way, in treatment as well. Most treatment programs in the United States teach patients to become involved in twelve-step recovery, a support system that continues long after one has left formal treatment. Most of my patients report that, although they attended meetings in treatment, they became actively involved in twelve-step recovery *after* they left treatment. Alcoholics Anonymous (A.A.), Narcotics Anonymous (N.A.), Cocaine Anonymous (C.A.), Al-Anon, Nar-Anon, and Overeaters Anonymous (O.A.) all provide structure and a place to belong. These meetings do not preach religion; however, most members see the change of twelve-step recovery as a spiritual experience.

The process of transformation and recovery has been known since the 1930s. Alcoholics Anonymous, started by Bill Wilson and Dr. Bob Smith, has saved the lives of millions of people dependent on the drug alcohol. In the 1960s, people who were intensely addicted to drugs other than alcohol gathered together to form Narcotics Anonymous. N.A. was based on the principles of Alcoholics Anonymous. More recently, in many cities, cocaine dependent people have banded together to create Cocaine Anonymous. These twelve-step programs hold the central key to the transformation process known as recovery. This book does not replace twelve-step programs. Rather, this book is a supplement to the twelve-step recovery process. To be completely removed from the Cocaine Addiction Cycle one must walk a path of recovery.

Recovery is a reflex of the mind that occurs with active involvement on the addict's part. This involvement is not driven by intellect or curiosity. It is an involvement of the heart, of the emotions, and of the soul. Recovery requires a rearrangement of almost every aspect of an addict's life.

FOUR

Detoxification

Principles

1. Cocaine withdrawal is not life threatening; therefore detoxification medications are not an absolute necessity.

2. When cocaine is introduced to the brain, it modifies the chemical communication between nerve cells.

3. Cocaine alters nerve cell functioning in the reward center of the brain, producing the initial sense of reward and the subsequent compulsive craving for the drug.

4. The medical detoxification for cocaine addiction strives to correct the biochemical abnormalities produced during cocaine use.

5. Cocaine toxicity influences how addicts see the world around them and their place in the world. Addicts are peculiarly blind to how cocaine has affected their minds.

Cocaine causes many toxic effects on the brain. Being *detoxified* from cocaine means just that, eliminating the toxic effects of cocaine on the brain and the body. Each treatment program for cocaine dependence has a different philosophy concerning the detoxification process. Many treatment programs place all cocaine addicts on detoxification medications early in the treatment of cocaine dependency. The detoxification compounds are given to neutralize the toxic effects of cocaine on the mind and body. Other treatment centers rarely, if ever, use medical agents of any sort in the treatment of cocaine dependency. A third type of treatment center occupies the middle ground between these two extremes, using medications in some cases of cocaine dependence but allowing the mind to clear without medications in others. I will describe the three major philosophies of cocaine detoxification below. It is important to understand that no single method of detoxification has been proven by research to be significantly better than another.

This chapter will describe some of the current scientific data on cocaine and its effects on the body. Then I will discuss several of the detoxification protocols that arise out of this information. Once this chapter has been read, it may be helpful to discuss the information with a physician.

Principle 1 — Cocaine withdrawal is not life threatening; therefore detoxification medications are not an absolute necessity.

When an alcohol or sedative addict uses daily, he becomes physically dependent on his drugs. If the drug is discontinued completely, the body may react violently—often with delirium tremens or seizures. Cocaine does not cause these obvious physical withdrawal problems such as blood pressure problems or shakes. Researchers in the past noted that cocaine withdrawal caused no physical withdrawal complications, and so they summarily decided that cocaine withdrawal did not exist. In the 1960s, physicians and researchers equated the presence of physical withdrawal with a drug's addictive potential. Because cocaine was believed to have no withdrawal symptoms, it was declared to be *nonaddicting!*

Drug craving, depression, agitation, and the cocaine-induced distortions about life are the complications of acute and chronic cocaine consumption. How an addict thinks and feels in the early stages of coming off cocaine *is* cocaine withdrawal. Cocaine withdrawal is severe; it affects addicts in the most complex and least understood part of the body—the brain.

The confusion about the effects of cocaine on the body and the mind has created many different approaches to the detoxification of cocaine addicted people. Some treatment programs advocate using good nutrition as the only medical treatment for cocaine withdrawal. These treatment programs believe that medications are drugs, and drugs of any sort are deleterious for an individual who is drug dependent. Addicts early in recovery tend to hang on to any chemical, hoping it will eliminate their addiction. Using chemicals in the detoxification process may send a mixed message to the recovering addict. The confusing message is, "Drugs fix drug addiction." In its worst form, patients may perceive that if they use the detoxification medications long enough, they will recover from cocaine dependency without any additional effort. They believe, "Pills fix problems." Nothing could be further from the truth. Conservative programs feel that they need to avoid collusion with this notion. These treatment programs advocate total abstinence from pills, some even to the point of avoiding vitamin supplementation. Conservative programs stress behavioral, cognitive, social, and spiritual tools for recovery that are taught and experienced in the treatment process.

Reformative treatment programs advocate giving some patients antidepressants or other medications to combat the depression and the agitation that occur during detoxification. These programs believe that the agitation and depression prevent the patient from becoming involved in treatment. These programs worry that a patient may miss some important information or experience in treatment if he is experiencing drug craving, agitation, or mood problems. They consider the use of sedatives, antidepressants, or mood stabilizers such as lithium carbonate helpful, or at the very least, a necessary evil.

A third detoxification philosophy occupies the middle ground between the reformative and the conservative. Programs in the middle ground employ a range of detoxification medications and approaches. The detoxification process varies for each patient, according to severity of the cocaine dependence and the personality of the patient. Some patients have used pills to adjust to their problems for such a long time that they would see the use of any detoxification medications as fixing the addiction. Other patients are very toxic from the effects of cocaine and troubled by cocaine cravings. These

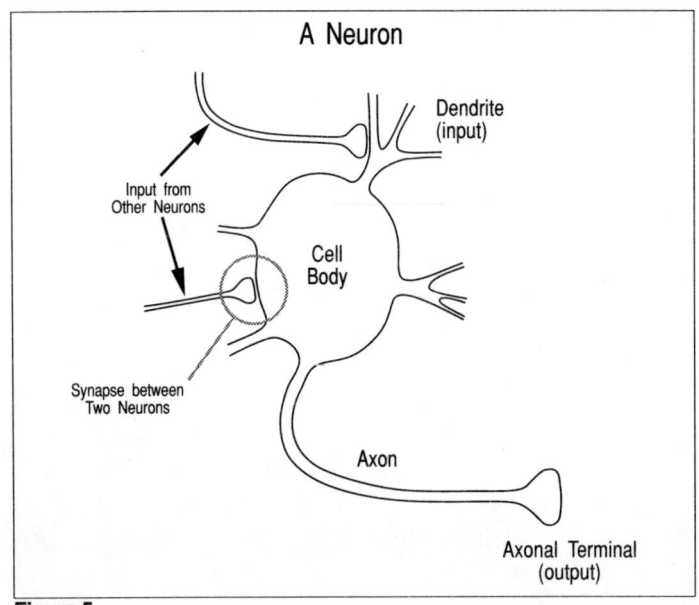

Figure 5
The neuron is the basic unit of information-processing in the brain. The dendrites accept input, which is then processed by the cell. The response, an electrical discharge, is sent down the axon, and on to the next nerve cell.

patients may need anti-craving agents to enable them to participate in treatment. They benefit from correcting the biochemical abnormalities cocaine has created on their unsuspecting brains.

How does cocaine affect the brain and the mind? How does it drive an addict to use over and over again, despite dire consequences? How does detoxification help correct the toxic effects of cocaine on the mind? To answer these questions, I will first examine how the brain uses chemicals to communicate. Then I will explore how cocaine is believed to affect the chemistry of communication in the brain. With this data, it will be possible to understand how to correct the neurochemical complications of cocaine addiction.

Detoxification

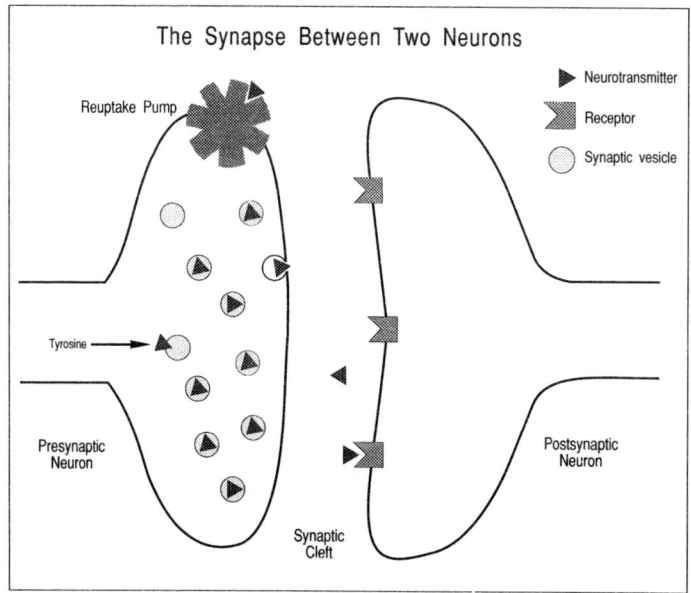

Figure 6
The junction of two nerve cells is called a synapse. When a presynaptic cell needs to signal a postsynaptic cell, it discharges packets of neurotransmitters (chemicals) that travel between cells (in the synaptic cleft). These neurotransmitters are sensed by postsynaptic receptors on the second nerve cell. Once they have completed their mission, used neurotransmitters are pumped back into the presynaptic cell and recycled for future communications.

The Neurochemistry of Cocaine

Much is known about how cocaine affects the brain. In fact, researchers know more about how cocaine modifies brain activity than about how alcohol actually functions in the brain. The exact mechanisms of the addiction process and the full nature of the effect of cocaine on the brain are, as yet, unclear. The reader should be aware that the information in this book is up to date and accurate for the year 1990. Future research will improve our understanding of cocaine addiction.

The brain is comprised of billions of small nerve cells called neurons. Each neuron processes information. It is the summation of the information processing by each of the billions of neurons that creates the vast array of our brain's activity. A small portion of this activity results in our conscious thoughts and feelings. Each neuron receives information through chemical messages, processes this information, and then creates an electrical discharge. The electrical discharge is carried down a length of that nerve cell called the axon. The information is, in this manner, passed down these axonal wires by an electrical discharge (see Figure 5). When the signal reaches the end of that nerve cell, it is not sent to the next nerve cell by electrical conduction. Rather, information is passed from cell to cell by messenger chemicals, known as neurotransmitters. The communication between neurons occurs when a neurotransmitter from one cell is detected by a second cell.

When the electrical signal arrives at the end of the first cell, it causes that cell to discharge a minute quantity of a specific neurotransmitter. Each nerve cell communicates by using only one of the many known neurotransmitters. The neurotransmitter, once released, drifts away from the first cell, known as the presynaptic neuron, and moves across an extremely small space known as the synaptic cleft (see Figure 6). When the neurotransmitters encounter the next nerve cell, they are sensed by specific receptors on the second nerve cell (the postsynaptic neuron). The communication time between nerve cells is very short, because the gap between the two cells is so tiny. The neurotransmitters cross the synaptic cleft and are sensed by the postsynaptic neuron in a fraction of a thousandth of one second.

If a sufficient quantity of chemicals from the first cell reaches the second cell across the synaptic cleft, they create an electrical discharge in the postsynaptic nerve cell.[2] In this way, information is processed, and sent through the brain. The signal from a first (presynaptic) cell is usually reviewed along with other signals from other input cells by the postsynaptic

---

2. Neuro transmitters are divided into two basic types: excitatory and inhibitory. The majority of neurotransmitters are actually inhibitory, they function to keep the postsynaptic cell from discharging. Others induce the postsynaptic neuron to fire, and are thus called excitatory.

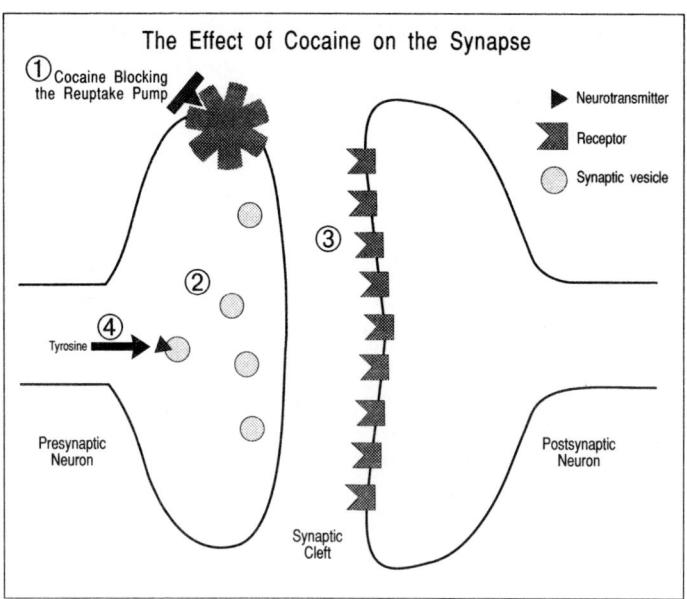

Figure 7
Cocaine produces changes in the brain by affecting the synapse. Cocaine has four effects on the synapse: 1. It blocks the neurotransmitter reuptake pump; 2. It depletes the neurotransmitters dopamine and norepinephrine; 3. The number of postsynaptic receptor sites are increased; 4. The rate of synthesis of dopamine is increased.

cell. If the second cell senses enough neurotransmitter from the many input cells, it will respond as well. The cumulative effect of many cells sending information to a processing nerve cell establishes information processing in the brain. All of the activities we think of as brain activity, such as thought, vision, movement, speech, and perception of music, are all an accumulation of various quantities of electrical discharges combined with the passage or blockage of these discharges from one nerve cell to the next.

Once a given neurotransmitter has created its effect on the postsynaptic neuron, it is either destroyed (metabolized) or it is reabsorbed into the presynaptic cell to be packaged and reused. The brain is very consistent in how it processes used neurotransmitters. Most neurotransmitters involved in the effect of cocaine are reabsorbed into the presynaptic cell. A pump between the synaptic cleft (where the used neurotransmitters are sitting) and the presynaptic cell terminal moves the used neurotransmitters back into the effector (presynaptic) cell. This permits these chemicals to be used to send messages again. A diagram of the reuptake pump is depicted in Figure 6. The reabsorption process is quite efficient; it prevents the body from having to remanufacture chemicals for successive brain signals that number in the trillions per minute! Excess neurotransmitters that are not reabsorbed float about the brain substance and are destroyed or metabolized by enzymes in the brain.

Principle 2 — When cocaine is introduced to the brain it modifies the chemical communication between nerve cells.

Three of these neurotransmitter chemicals—dopamine, norepinephrine, and serotonin—are implicated in the effect of cocaine on the brain. Cocaine creates its effect on brain function by modifying the transmission of electrical impulses in several ways. Clear evidence indicates that cocaine works, to a large extent, by blocking the reuptake or reabsorption of the neurotransmitters dopamine, norepinephrine, and serotonin into the presynaptic nerve cell. Cocaine fouls the reuptake pump that moves the neurotransmitters from the synaptic cleft back into the presynaptic cell. When the reuptake pump is fouled, the neurotransmitters released by normal nerve cell activity remain in the synaptic cleft between the cells, temporarily increasing the quantity of neurotransmitters in the synaptic cleft. The increased quantity of neurotransmitters, in turn, increases the stimulation of the postsynaptic nerve cell. This stimulation causes the postsynaptic cell to fire repeatedly. Thus, the major effect of cocaine on the brain is to cause very rapid firing of some neurons in the brain.

Principle 3 — Cocaine alters nerve cell functioning in the reward center of the brain, producing the initial sense of reward and the subsequent compulsive craving for the drug.

Because cocaine causes rapid firing in many dopamine, norepinephrine, and serotonin neurons of the brain, this effect on some brain areas is more pronounced than on others.

Detoxification

When the neurons in the reward center fire rapidly, the animal or human is overcome with a sensation of reward. This occurs when cocaine is administered to a brain that has not been subjected to cocaine before, a so-called *naive brain*. The cocaine user is looking for this effect. Cocaine short circuits our natural reward mechanisms, stimulating a reward sensation directly in the reward center.

The reward center quickly adjusts to the effects of cocaine. This adjustment decreases the intensity of the reward upon each subsequent drug binge. It also decreases the sense of reward with repeated cocaine use during a given binge. Therefore, when the user consumes his first hit at the start of a binge, he experiences the greatest reward or high. If he uses again, hoping for the same effect, he feels much less euphoria. This frustrates the addict and drives him to use more cocaine in a vain effort to recapture his first high.

Cocaine affects many other areas of the brain as well. The stimulation of other areas creates the side effects of cocaine, including: motor acceleration, muscle cramping, thought acceleration, rapid disorganized thought, seizures, sleeplessness, lack of hunger, and several additional effects. Other parts of the brain develop a tolerance to the effects of cocaine more slowly than the reward center. For example, the arousal areas of the brain, when their reuptake pumps are blocked by cocaine, cause the user to be alert. As drug consumption continues, the user feels hyper-alert. This proceeds to paranoia and often visual or auditory hallucinations. Even though the reward system stops responding to cocaine, the hyper-alertness, the paranoia, and the hallucinations do not habituate as easily. Thus the cocaine user expects to obtain a feeling of reward, but instead experiences paranoia, anxiety, depression, and sleeplessness.

Cocaine stimulates the motor areas of the brain in a similar fashion. This creates the pacing, rapid speech, and increased muscle tone during drug use. The motor areas in the deeper parts of the brain also create the repeated, seemingly senseless automatic movements (twitches and motor tics) under cocaine's effects. The increase in muscle tone results in muscle aches in the back, calves, and jaws following a cocaine binge. This increased muscle tone can also stimulate a sustained muscular contraction resulting in muscle injury. Blood samples drawn after a binge may report damage to muscle fiber as a result of cocaine use.

Cocaine also blocks the reuptake pump of neurons in the sleep induction center of the brain. When the sleep induction center is blocked, it cannot induce sleep. The cocaine user suffers with agitated insomnia after using cocaine. The sleep center rebounds when all the cocaine in the body is metabolized. This rebound drives the addict to sleep in Stage III of the Cocaine Addiction Cycle. Cocaine addicts often develop unusual sleep patterns once they are inducted into the Cocaine Addiction Cycle. The addict's sleep pattern alternates between long periods of little sleep and periods of fatigue and sleep for 10 to 14 hours at a time.

When cocaine stimulates the brain, it frequently causes seizures. As noted above, the major effect of cocaine on the brain is to increase nerve cell firing. The uncontrolled increase in nerve cell firing enlists unrelated neighboring nerve cells to discharge in synchrony. If enough nerve cells in a given area discharge together, a localized seizure occurs. If this small group of cells, in turn, recruits a synchronous discharge in larger portions of the brain, the drug user experiences a grand mal seizure that results in a loss of consciousness. If a person is using cocaine while performing a dangerous activity—such as driving—he risks an accident. A grand mal cocaine seizure can also cause heart irregularity and even heart stoppage.

When most people think of seizures, they envision the entire body jerking in convulsions. Seizures do not, however, always result in the entire body and brain convulsing. Localized synchronous electrical discharges from a group of nerve cells result in partial seizures. Partial seizures may cause a variety of bizarre sensory and muscle movements. Unfortunately, the brain learns to have seizures as it learns any other brain activity. If a cocaine user has a single seizure, he is exposing himself to a double danger. The first danger is the seizure itself. The second, more ominous danger is that the addict's brain may learn to have additional seizures after having had the first. The process of learning to have seizures is called *kindling*. Cocaine use kindles the brain to be seizure prone. This kindled state is thought to last a lifetime, long after cocaine use stops.

A single dose of cocaine increases the concentration of neurotransmitters in the synaptic cleft. If the reuptake pump is blocked by cocaine, what then happens to these neurotransmitters? These chemicals move slowly into the substance of the brain and are metabolized (destroyed) by enzymes. As noted above, the nerve cells involved with cocaine are based on *a reuptake economy*. This means that nerve cells will have a sufficient quantity of neurotransmitters only if the reuptake pump recycles used neurotransmitters. If the reuptake pump is blocked, the pump is unable to resupply the presynaptic neuron. The neglected neurotransmitters begin to drift away from the synapse only to be metabolized in other areas of the brain. Thus, the level of available dopamine, norepinephrine, and serotonin in the brain falls. This rebound drop in available dopamine, norepinephrine, and serotonin generates the cocaine crash. The drug user consumes cocaine to obtain the high created by excess neurotransmitters in the synaptic cleft. This short-term effect is offset by the long-term depletion of these chemicals. The depletion of dopamine, norepinephrine, and serotonin makes the user feel depressed, unrewarded, and hopeless. The level of all three neurotransmitters rises during a cocaine binge. This is followed by a prolonged drop in available dopamine, norepinephrine, and serotonin. Once addicted, the cocaine user incurs the exact opposite effect that he wanted from the cocaine. When he expects euphoria, he feels depression. When he expects stimulation and excitation, he becomes apathetic and sleepy.

The postsynaptic cells respond to this neurotransmitter depletion by increasing their sensitivity to the needed neurotransmitters. The postsynaptic cells increase their sensitivity by manufacturing additional receptors. The degree of receptor increase has been correlated with the degree of drug craving—that is, a marked increase in the number of dopamine receptors causes intense drug craving in early recovery. This hypothesis was first reported by Drs. Dackis and Gold in 1985 (see *Additional Readings*). Through chronic cocaine use, the addict has depleted his stores of neurotransmitters, and increased the sensitivity of his postsynaptic receptors in many areas of the brain. This results in depression and drug craving. See Figure 7 for a summary of the changes induced by cocaine.

Principle 4 — The medical detoxification for cocaine addiction strives to correct the biochemical abnormalities produced during cocaine use.

Detoxification of the addict attempts to reverse each of the biochemical consequences of chronic cocaine use. Detoxification aspires to return the brain to its original state. The medications and vitamin supplements aim at each of the side effects induced by cocaine use. Cocaine causes many abnormalities in brain functioning, including:

- An increase in the number of dopamine and norepinephrine receptors on some neurons in the brain.
- A depletion of the neurotransmitters dopamine, norepinephrine, and probably serotonin.
- An increase in the synthesis (production) rate of dopamine and norepinephrine.
- Vitamin deficiencies, especially in the B-complex vitamins (Pyridoxine and Thiamine, most notably), folic acid, and Vitamin C.

Treatment for cocaine toxicity should first and foremost correct the known effects of cocaine on the brain. Other medications may prove helpful, but addicts should be cautious about consuming any medications that may produce a substitute dependency.

Detoxification medications can be divided into two types: those that address the known toxic effects of cocaine and those that may prove helpful for other reasons. I will discuss medications and supplements that address the known toxic effects of cocaine first.

Table 1 - Primary medications used in cocaine detoxification

Medication	Presumed effect
Bromocriptine (Parlodel®)	Decreases drug craving, decreases neurotransmitter sensitivity.
Amantadine (Symmetrel®)	Increases the release of dopamine from neurons in the brain.
L-tyrosine, L-phenylalanine	Increases stores of dopamine and norepinephrine.
B-complex and Vitamin C	Factors necessary to manufacture neurotransmitters.

The most common medication used to reverse the toxic effects of cocaine is bromocriptine (Parlodel®). Bromocriptine was first discovered to be effective in cocaine addicted individuals by Drs. Mark Gold and Charles Dackis. These investigators found that bromocriptine decreased cocaine cravings. They tested the craving level of addicts by exposing them to pictures of cocaine and cocaine apparatus. These patients then described their level of cocaine craving. The patients were then given bromocriptine or a placebo. Bromocriptine was found to reduce the level of craving induced by such visual cues. Neurochemical research has found that bromocriptine occupies or sits on the dopamine receptors (see Figure 6). Drug craving is decreased when bromocriptine attaches to postsynaptic dopamine receptors. The use of bromocriptine over time is also thought to decrease the number of postsynaptic dopamine receptors as well. By reducing the number of postsynaptic receptors, the reward center in the brain is restored to a pre-cocaine state.

Bromocriptine, in the low doses used in cocaine dependent patients, has very few side effects. Among the side effects noted are light headedness or dizziness, occasional nausea and, rarely, vomiting. In higher doses, bromocriptine has been known to have long-term side effects. However, none of these have been reported in the short-term detoxification of cocaine dependent patients. This medication is usually given two to three times a day early in recovery and is administered for a period of five days to four weeks.

Other medications that modify the communication between dopaminergic nerve cells (neurons that communicate through the use of dopamine) have been used in the treatment of cocaine dependence. The second medication listed in Table 1 is amantadine (Symmetrel®). Amantadine is given to cocaine addicts shortly after entering treatment and in a manner similar to bromocriptine. Although the mechanism of action of this medication is less precisely known, it appears to promote the release of dopamine from the presynaptic neurons in the brain. As stated above, cocaine depletes the stores of dopamine in presynaptic neurons. Therefore, amantadine may be attempting to release dopamine that simply is not there. Using amantadine in cocaine detoxification does not follow our current biochemical logic for the treatment of cocaine cravings. Several published studies, however, have indicated that amantadine may be helpful in cocaine withdrawal.[3] These reports point out the uncertainty in our understanding of how cocaine works in the human brain.

Cocaine depletes the brain's neurotransmitters by blocking reuptake of the chemicals dopamine, norepinephrine, and serotonin. When reuptake blockade occurs, these neurotransmitters drift away from the presynaptic cells where they are needed. The neurotransmitters enter the substance of the brain, and there they are broken down. This metabolism prevents neurotransmitters from stimulating the wrong neurons in other areas of the brain. The metabolism of these chemicals decreases the levels of dopamine, norepinephrine, and serotonin in the brain.

---

3. See the work of Tennant and others. One reference appears in *Additional Readings* at the end of Part Two.

Thus, after using cocaine for a short time, the addict winds up decreasing his stores of vital neurotransmitters. These neurotransmitters are necessary to regulate sleep, to stimulate a sense of reward, and to engender a sense of well-being.

Neurotransmitters are synthesized in the brain itself from amino acids. Amino acids are supplied to the brain by food. When one eats protein, the stomach and the small intestine break down proteins into amino acids. The amino acids are absorbed into the bloodstream and are carried throughout the body. The brain absorbs its needed amino acids from the blood stream. In the brain, amino acids are converted into various compounds. Among the most important of these are the neurotransmitters dopamine, norepinephrine, and serotonin.

Cocaine use depletes dopamine and norepinephrine and, at the same time, turns up the synthetic machinery for these neurotransmitters. The brain's machinery attempts to offset the depleting effects of cocaine. The administration of the precursor amino acids L-phenylalanine or L-tyrosine helps to drive the synthesis of dopamine and norepinephrine. When a person eats protein, or takes amino acid supplements, he is supplying needed precursors for the manufacture of neurotransmitters depleted by cocaine. For this reason, some detoxification protocols use the precursor amino acids L-phenylalanine or L-tyrosine as a nutritional supplement and as a pharmacological boost to the synthesis of these neurotransmitters.

The side effects of L-phenylalanine and L-tyrosine are negligible. People who have had the skin cancer *melanoma* should avoid using these amino acids. People who are taking Monoamine Oxidase Inhibitors (a type of antidepressant medication) should also avoid taking them. Large doses of L-tyrosine can decrease blood pressure in some patients and large doses of L-phenylalanine can increase blood pressure to a small degree. Patients who have failure of their kidneys or liver need to be careful in their use of these compounds. The relative incidence of side effects from these precursors, however, is exceedingly small.

A third amino acid, L-tryptophan, is used by the brain as a precursor for serotonin. The serotonin reuptake pump is also blocked by cocaine. Because of reuptake blockade, the cocaine affected brain sees an initial increase in serotonin, followed by a prolonged serotonin depletion subsequent to a cocaine binge. This rise and fall in serotonin level is comparable to the rise and fall in dopamine and norepinephrine levels during a cocaine binge. Like L-phenylalanine and L-tyrosine, L-tryptophan must be obtained by eating protein. Unlike dopamine and norepinephrine, however, serotonin synthesis is not increased by cocaine usage. This provides less compelling evidence that diet supplementation of L-tryptophan will speed the replacement of serotonin in the brain.

Until recently, treatment centers administered L-tryptophan in pharmacologic doses hoping to increase serotonin levels in recovering addicts' brains. In the fall of 1989, several medical centers reported a complication from the use of commercially available L-tryptophan. This complication, known as Eosinophilia-myalgia, was severe enough to warrant the recall of all supplements that contained L-tryptophan. Since that time, the danger of Eosinophilia-myalgia has been traced to contaminants in the manufacturing process of L-tryptophan. However, L-tryptophan, as of this writing, has not been approved for re-release in the United States. Instead, we rely on food proteins to supplement the diet of cocaine addicts with needed L-tryptophan during the detoxification process.

Vitamin supplements are the last medication listed in Table 1. Cocaine addicts often develop multiple vitamin deficiencies. Despite the fact that most cocaine addicts periodically eat large amounts of food (especially in Stage III), they rarely eat balanced diets. Malnutrition occurs when poor eating habits are combined with the stressful demands cocaine places on the body.

In one group of patients entering a treatment center, clinicians reported specific Vitamin B, Vitamin C, and folic acid deficiencies. Vitamins play an essential role in the reconstruction of the cocaine ravaged brain. A balanced diet should begin to repair the cocaine-induced damage. This diet is frequently supplemented with a multivitamin including the B-complex vitamins: Thiamine (B_1), Riboflavin (B_2), Pyridoxine (B_6), Cyanocobalamin (B_{12}), and Niacin. Vitamin B-complex tablets usually contain Pantothenic Acid. Vitamin supplementation corrects deficiencies and may help supply vital nutrients for the normalization of the recovering brain. Many clinicians prescribe a therapeutic dosage of Vitamin B-complex with Vitamin C and folic acid for all cocaine addicts in the first two months of recovery.

Other medications such as tricyclic antidepressants and carbamazepine may help detoxify or permit the mind to understand treatment as well. Although the specific neurochemical effect of these medications in cocaine withdrawal is not known, one should not conclude that they are without benefit. Because of side effects, incomplete data, or mood altering effects, I do consider these medications to be less central in the treatment of cocaine addiction.

Table 2 - Secondary medications used in cocaine detoxification

Medication	Presumed effect
Carbamazepine (Tegretol®)	Decreases craving and treatment drop-out, decreases cocaine consumption.
Tricyclic antidepressants	Decrease depression, may decrease treatment drop-out.

Recent research by Dr. James Halikas at the University of Minnesota has suggested that another medication, carbamazepine (Tegretol®), may be helpful in the treatment of cocaine addiction. Long-term cocaine addicts will decrease their cocaine consumption (some will even stop using cocaine entirely) when they are given carbamazepine. When given to cocaine addicts, carbamazepine will increase treatment compliance and decrease cocaine craving. Carbamazepine is an effective antiseizure medication; this has led researchers to speculate that cocaine craving is a type of localized brain seizure. Although preliminary at this time, the research using carbamazepine in cocaine addicts looks quite promising. Because carbamazepine is not a psychoactive drug, it seems well suited to abstinence-based recovery.

After stopping cocaine, many patients feel depressed. This depression may be evidenced by blue feelings, a lack of energy, poor appetite, and sleeping difficulties. More commonly, people who have stopped using cocaine report a different type of depression, consisting of high and undirected energy, a restless feeling, and anhedonia. Anhedonia is a feeling that things have ceased to give pleasure. Cocaine addicts report, "The things I used to do for pleasure don't seem to mean much to me anymore." This is characteristic of the anhedonic depression caused by cocaine withdrawal. This restlessness, high energy, and anhedonic depression is often mistaken by both treatment personnel and the patient as *being in a good mood.* Most addicts in recovery for more than six months look back on the first ninety days of recovery as a time of confusion and emptiness.

This restless, cocaine-induced depression is striking. It has encouraged some researchers and clinicians to use antidepressant medications in the treatment of cocaine dependence. Antidepressant medications increase available dopamine, norepinephrine, and serotonin in nerve cells in brain areas that regulate mood. This may stabilize mood problems in patients who have a cocaine-induced depression. The most common antidepressants do, however, cause sleepiness and seem to slow patients down. They also require between two and four weeks to be effective. Giving antidepressants to a cocaine addict may convince him that his *real* problem is depression (see the section on Denial in Chapter 6). For these reasons, antidepressants should be used with caution in recovering cocaine addicts. In addition, the therapeutic effect of most antidepressants begins after three weeks and maximizes at six weeks or more. Therefore, antidepressant medications may not help with the depression that occurs in the first month of recovery.

Antidepressants may have actions on the cocaine toxic brain other than improving mood. In well-designed studies, the empiric administration of antidepressants to cocaine addicts has been shown to decrease the amount of cocaine an addict consumes. This research has been interpreted by many physicians to indicate that tricyclic antidepressants are helpful in the withdrawal process from cocaine. Most of the research on the use of antidepressants for cocaine addiction was conducted in treatment settings where patients were not abstinent from addicting drugs. Such research may or may not be applicable to individuals who are in treatment programs that stress complete drug abstinence.

Tricyclic antidepressants have frequent but minor side effects. Some of the complications of these antidepressant medications may include dry mouth, palpitations of the heart, constipation, and—in some individuals—a sleepy or lethargic feeling. These medications are most frequently administered at night to reduce the consequence of sleepiness. At effective doses, antidepressants may create a fine tremor. In rare instances with patients who have bipolar disease (manic-depressive illness), these medications may worsen their condition. Caution must be used in prescribing these medications for the elderly or for people who suffer from heart problems. Antidepressants are dangerous if consumed in large quantities, either accidently or intentionally. Used as prescribed, however, antidepressant medications are generally quite safe.

Cocaine Toxicity

Principle 5 — Cocaine toxicity influences how addicts see the world and their place in the world. Addicts are peculiarly blind to how cocaine has affected their minds.

People who use cocaine feel only minor physical effects after discontinuing a cocaine binge. Cocaine causes no physical signs of withdrawal, no shakes or tremors, no hallucinations, and no changes in pulse, body temperature, or blood pressure. This has caused many addicts to say things like: "I'm psychologically dependent on cocaine, but not addicted." They sense that they are in trouble, but because they can go days at a time without using the drug, they believe their cocaine habit is not a *real addiction*. Patients early in treatment often ask me, "Why am I in detoxification?" They do not feel that there is any toxicity resulting from their cocaine use. The most troublesome part of cocaine toxicity is that it is pervasive; it blinds the addict from seeing that anything is wrong.

To work his way out of toxicity's reflexive blindness, the addict must visualize himself in the Cocaine Addiction Cycle. How he uses cocaine constitutes his unique addiction cycle. By seeing himself in this cycle, the addict distances himself from his distorted thinking. As he recovers from the last binge, the addict develops a deceptive sense of well-being. This feeling of well-being in Stage IV does not mean, however, that the addict is unaffected by his cocaine usage.

Most of the toxic effects of cocaine are localized in the brain. The Cocaine Addiction Cycle, the post-cocaine depression, and the cocaine cravings are all manifestations of withdrawal. Detoxification from cocaine is, in fact, quite prolonged and troublesome. People around the addict can discern when his behavior is determined by cocaine withdrawal. The addict cannot.

Table 3 - The components of cocaine brain toxicity

Time from last use	Effect on cocaine user
4 to 48 hours	Depression and remorse
1 to 15 days	Hyperexcitability
2 to 40 days	Returning sense of control
2 to 40 days	Grandiosity
2 days to 2 years	Intermittent intense cocaine craving
10 to 90 days	Anhedonia

Cocaine toxicity can be divided into six components. The first component is the depression and remorse felt during

Stage II of the addiction cycle. Depression is treated by therapy; there the patient can discuss his feelings and losses in life. This depression quickly dissipates as it is replaced by other components of cocaine toxicity.

The second component occurs as the depression lifts and the addict moves into Stage IV. Here, patients feel a return of nervous energy, a restless feeling that keeps them from being able to concentrate. Most addicts become hyperexcitable, feeling at times like caged lions. Excitability is, strangely enough, at its worst when patients are feeling the most empty about their lives. The restlessness seems to peak seven to ten days after the last cocaine use, and may prompt patients to leave treatment. Exercise is most helpful to patients during these restless times. It has proven to be an important adjunctive element in the treatment of cocaine addiction. Activity is best interspersed with psychotherapy. When healthy exercise patterns continue after treatment, they decrease the probability of relapse. Therefore, I recommend that patients in recovery develop a lifestyle that includes frequent aerobic exercise. If an addict exercises routinely, the excitability decreases after the first two weeks of abstinence.

The third component of cocaine toxicity is a returning sense of self-control. During a binge, addicts feel out of control, unable to manage their behaviors. Several days after stopping cocaine, addicts begin to feel that they are once again in control of their lives. After all, they stopped using! This sense of control is a cognitive (thinking) distortion created by cocaine. Patients in early recovery need to constantly remind themselves of their lack of control over cocaine, and their lack of control over their lives as a result of addiction. Fellow addicts can help point out that the patient's sense of self-control is an illusion.

The fourth component of cocaine toxicity is grandiosity. Grandiosity is often apparent in such statements as "I can handle this on my own" and "I'm not like other cocaine users." These statements are made at a time when the addict is very ill from his cocaine usage. It is obvious to everyone else around him that he is as ill as anyone else and cannot discontinue his cocaine habit on his own. Cocaine-induced grandiosity is best confronted by staff and fellow patients in a treatment setting. Confronting grandiosity is confronting the disease of addiction, not the addict himself.

A fifth component of cocaine toxicity is cocaine craving. Craving occurs in many forms and is correlated with the length of time from the last drug use. Drug craving is dealt with first and foremost by acknowledging that it exists. If an addict does not tell others about his drug cravings or feels badly about himself for having drug cravings, the drug cravings only become worse. The next chapter provides a complete discussion of drug craving.

The sixth component of drug toxicity is anhedonia, a feeling that life holds very little meaning. This is accompanied by a sense of inner emptiness. Anhedonia makes life's goals seem pointless, a marked contrast to the intense euphoria that was once created by cocaine. If an addict understands that many of life's goals will seem empty or flat for a period of time, he will be less troubled. During the period of anhedonia, an individual may make poor decisions about his life due to the perceived emptiness of his previous goals. Anhedonia may last as long as one year, but always leaves in time.

FIVE

Cocaine Craving Patterns

Principles

1. Cocaine craving is a learned response to cocaine use.

2. There are four types of cocaine craving: reinforced-use, overt, covert, and conditioned-cue craving.

3. Covert craving appears directly on the heels of resolving overt craving.

When a drug user has decided to stop cocaine, many obstacles stand in his way. The largest obstacle to abstinence is cocaine craving. Drug craving is the most troublesome and frequent complication that results from cocaine addiction. Craving appears randomly and can completely interrupt a recovering addict's daily activities. Craving makes the addict feel as if cocaine use is imminent. Some people experience relentless daily cocaine craving. Others are only occasionally bothered by craving. Despite its random nature, cocaine craving is distracting and, at its worst, life threatening. Cocaine craving frequently results in relapse.

In this chapter, I will discuss the four types of drug craving and how each is generated, and introduce specific coping skills for each type of craving. The reader may want to read about each type of craving and follow this with the related exercises in *The Cocaine Recovery Workbook*. The workbook is designed to help with individual craving patterns.

Principle 1 — Cocaine craving is a learned response to cocaine use.

Cocaine creates two types of neurophysiological change that initiate drug craving. During the initial experience with cocaine, the mind feels intense euphoria and stimulation. The memory of the euphoric episode during cocaine use creates the first change—a specific *cocaine tape.* Cocaine tapes are imprinted memories in the brain. The memory of cocaine use floats through the mind in the same manner as any other memory. Following the euphoria comes the cocaine crash. The user feels anxious and depressed during the crash. The mind senses this depression and wants to escape from this feeling. The drive to escape cocaine-induced depression produces the second change. Both changes combine to create craving. For unknown reasons, these two effects are not otherwise connected in the brain. That is, the addict's brain does not learn that cocaine use will be followed by cocaine crash. When the addict thinks of cocaine use, he can only see as far as the initial high. He is driven to avoid his depression, and he knows that cocaine will make him temporarily happy. This peculiar type of short-sightedness, called *euphoric recall,* is characteristic of addicted persons.

Cocaine craving results from this type of learned response. Cocaine tapes, floating through the brain, are triggered by a stimulus in the brain (such as a thought) or by an external stimulus (seeing a picture of cocaine). The memories are unimpeded by the negative consequences of cocaine use and, therefore, create the sensations that the addict recognizes as drug craving.

Principle 2 — There are four types of cocaine craving: reinforced-use, overt, covert, and conditioned-cue craving.

Drug craving is a part of cocaine recovery, a side effect of long-term drug use. Drug craving comes in four distinct forms. Each form or type of drug craving has specific characteristics. Each craving pattern can be stopped through distinct interventions. Once an addict learns about each of these patterns and practices the techniques outlined in this chapter, he will reduce the probability that cravings will result in drug use. I will discuss each craving type separately.

Table 4 - The four types of cocaine craving

Craving type	Time seen	Characteristics
Reinforced-use	During cocaine use	Stopped only by lack of drug availability.
Overt interoceptive	1 to 20 days after last use	Triggered by body symptoms or thoughts. The addict is bothered by them and feels guilty about having them.
Covert	5 to 45 days after last use	Changes in behavior that indicate drug craving. The addict does not recognize them as cravings.
Conditioned-cue	14 days to 2 years after last use	Triggered by visual, smell, sound, or thought cue. The addict is troubled by them; they seem to be relentless.

Reinforced-Use Craving

The first type of craving is called *reinforced-use craving*. At the beginning of a cocaine binge (Stage I of the Cocaine Addiction Cycle, Figure 3), the addict plans to use a specific amount of cocaine. Shortly after the first hit or dose of the drug he becomes concerned about the quantity of cocaine he has available. He may think of hoarding some of the drug or protecting his supply from others. As more of the addict's supply is used, his panic level increases. Often the concern over the size of his supply consumes his thoughts. The anxiety over the loss of available cocaine pushes the addict to think of ways of obtaining more of the drug. The panic and compulsion to obtain more cocaine is produced by self-reinforcing craving from cocaine use. When deeply involved in his addiction, the addict often experiences craving for cocaine immediately after beginning cocaine consumption. This characteristic sets cocaine apart from other abused drugs. Cocaine is the only drug that *immediately* reinforces its own consumption.

The addict senses these self-reinforcing effects as *chasing one's tail* in an attempt to get higher. Cocaine addicts report that the only way to interrupt a cocaine binge is to have their access to the drug cutoff or to become physically exhausted. This is remarkably similar to how monkeys respond when they are given free access to cocaine. When driven by reinforced-use craving, the following will stop cocaine use:

- Lack of the drug and no source available, e.g., the dealer went to bed.
- Lack of the drug and no way of obtaining funds to buy more.
- Having friends physically remove the user from his cocaine supply.
- Complete exhaustion.

Not every cocaine user consumes cocaine up until one of these four points, some addicts have established using rituals that limit their drug intake. This is the exception, however, rather than the rule. People who have access to large quantities will use large quantities. Individuals who have large sums of money spend a larger amount than they can afford. Those who have little money spend it all. Reinforced-use craving drives some people to steal. Women and men exchange sexual favors for cocaine. These facts stress the importance of avoiding the first hit of cocaine. Stopping a full-blown relapse is nearly impossible after being exposed to a small quantity of cocaine. After the first hit, subsequent cocaine use is biologically driven by reinforced-use craving and is beyond the volitional control of most human beings.

Overt Interoceptive Craving

The second type of drug craving is called *overt interoceptive craving*. This type of craving is described as overt because the addict experiences the craving directly; he can label the experience as a desire to use cocaine. These cravings are defined as interoceptive because they are triggered by sensations in the body. This craving pattern occurs intermittently in Stage IV of the Cocaine Addiction Cycle and, if allowed to proceed, reaches a crescendo in Stage V.

Patients may feel high or under the influence of cocaine while experiencing overt interoceptive craving. These cravings are triggered by gastrointestinal discomfort, a racing pulse, a dry mouth, or sweaty palms; symptoms that precede the use of cocaine. Thoughts about a binge or a conversation with other users promotes these body experiences. Internal body experiences (interoceptive cues) reinforce the intensity of the cravings. These feelings then foster additional body sensations. This generates a vicious cycle; the cues foster feelings and thoughts, and these then generate more cues.

The following is an example of overt interoceptive craving. An addict in treatment participates in daily exercise—a basketball game with others. Because he is enjoying himself and out of shape, the exercise causes his heart to pound rapidly. The heart pounding (interoceptive cue) triggers strange feelings. The addict does not recognize these feelings as cravings to use cocaine. As he walks to his next activity, group therapy, he feels edgy and anticipatory. The anticipation is similar to the pre-cocaine jitters, feelings he would get prior to using cocaine (Stage V of the Cocaine Addiction Cycle). He then remembers that he had promised to speak about himself to the group today, and he feels increasing anxiety. His mouth begins to go dry and his palms may break out in a cold sweat. At this point he has a thought: "I want to use cocaine." The heart pounding, the anticipation, the sweaty palms, the dry mouth, and the anxiety all collide with each other, creating a strong urge to use cocaine. He goes to therapy but his body is ready to use.

Addicts cannot prevent overt interoceptive cravings from happening; they are outside the addict's control early in recovery. What then does an addict do when he finds himself having this kind of drug craving? First it should be determined what caused the craving to occur. The addict may trace it back to a singular event, something that was said, or a feeling inside his body. These events are then catalogued for future reference as craving triggers. In the example above, the heart racing from exercise was the trigger. This trigger was promoted to a craving episode by normal anxiety.

Once the trigger is established, it is important for the addict to describe briefly to others his craving episode: what triggered the craving, and what seems to be promoting his cocaine craving at that point. The addict should then stop and experience the craving with a supportive friend or a member of his treatment staff—describing the internal sensations while avoiding any elaboration on what he would do with this craving if he had cocaine. The addict must block himself from romanticizing thoughts of cocaine use. If he feels nervous, he should recall other times when he felt nervous, times that were unrelated to cocaine use. He should describe these times to those around him. After the addict has described his craving episode, he should move on to other activities. Thirty minutes to an hour later, he should attempt to recall the feelings brought on by the craving episode so he will remember what they are and that they do subside. Overt interoceptive craving episodes almost always remit in thirty minutes to one hour.

Prior to treatment, drug craving feels overpowering to addicts. They often believe the only way to make the cravings disappear is to use cocaine. While in treatment, the addict will experience the cravings again. It is critical to allow the process of drug craving to continue through to spontaneous remission. When an addict has completed treatment, he will again experience cocaine craving, but will be armed with craving management techniques and the knowledge that the craving will disappear spontaneously—if he does not use.

One of the most common reactions to cocaine craving is *drug romancing*. During his first craving episode in treatment, an addict frequently speaks about these feelings with his peers. The discussion moves from how the craving feels to talk of cocaine use. The conversation slowly deteriorates into war stories of past cocaine use. The addict has shifted from experiencing a craving episode to *drug romancing*. Drug romancing is different from craving: craving is a spontaneous internal event, while romancing is a self-induced elaboration in which drug use is seen as a positive experience, a grand adventure. Drug romancing is a way of accelerating and prolonging the craving, often generating a high caused by memories of past drug use. There is a subtle distinction between acknowledging the existence of drug craving and escalating the craving by romanticizing drug use. An addict may believe he is sharing how *awful it was* and switch very quickly into romanticizing his drug use. Therefore, it is important for an addict to experience cravings in a setting where other addicts or treatment staff will confront any drug romancing. Family and fellow addicts can help a cocaine addict discern the difference between drug romancing and drug craving. In the treatment environment, the addict will quickly learn that when an overt interoceptive craving appears, it is best for him to label and acknowledge the urge, process it, and move on.

During the time of overt interoceptive craving, an addict may also dream about using cocaine. These dreams are called, simply enough, *using dreams*. In the first of these dreams, the addict usually dreams of obtaining and preparing to use cocaine. Also in the first few dreams, patients describe experiencing the effect of cocaine (getting high). They often awake feeling a combination of disappointment—"I wish I could fall asleep and get high again"—and guilt—"Here I was in treatment; dreaming about using cocaine!" Each subsequent dream is filled with less and less cocaine euphoria and more and more guilt, panic, and cocaine crash. Cocaine dreams parallel the increasing comprehension of the negative consequences of cocaine use. Dreaming about cocaine is a normal part of recovery. As a person's time in recovery increases, the time between cocaine dreams will increase as well. Addicts in recovery for two to five years commonly continue to report occasional painful dreams about cocaine use; this too is a normal part of recovery.

Covert Craving

Principle 3 — Covert craving appears directly on the heels of resolving overt craving.

One of the ironies of cocaine recovery is that once an addict has mastered or understood overt interoceptive craving, it appears to vanish. Individuals who are seven to ten days into treatment often report to me that they are no longer experiencing drug craving. This period of decreasing overt craving is dangerous. Although the annoying overt cravings have gone, they are replaced by covert drug cravings. Covert cravings involve a feeling of restlessness in combination with a false sense of confidence that one will never be tempted to use again.

An example will best describe covert craving:

> A young man comes into treatment after two years of smoking cocaine. Each day for the first five days of treatment, he reports that he wants to use cocaine. During this time, he experiences periods of intense overt craving, with a rapid heart beat and sweaty palms. He talks with his fellow patients and with the staff whenever he experiences these craving episodes. Then, on the seventh day of treatment, he suddenly feels better. He reports that his cravings have dramatically decreased. He describes a feeling of "being back in control of himself." At the same time, his fellow patients remark that he seems fidgety and distracted. He brushes these confrontations aside, saying, "These people don't know me, anyway."
>
> The next day, the patient decides that he wants to leave treatment. When asked why he declares, "I have to go home and pay my bills." When informed that his wife has already paid the bills, he stammers and asserts that he has other reasons why he needs to discontinue treatment.

Why does he want to go? Is it because he feels he is not benefiting from treatment? Usually this is not the case. During the dangerous time of seven to twelve days after their last use, cocaine addicts *feel cured*. Feeling cured is one of the signs of Stage IV in the Cocaine Addiction Cycle. Often the addict will have very rational reasons to discontinue treatment, and will cite problems that have accumulated due to his cocaine use.

The patient's rationalizations for leaving treatment seem perfectly logical, but only to him. He feels he has things to do that are more important, not realizing that his major problem is dealing with the life or death issue of cocaine dependency.

Covert drug craving is a behavioral craving. The addict does not think or feel that cocaine use is imminent. Rather, his behavior is restless and he is easily excited. He feels in control, and that control tells him to move on. When asked directly if he intends to use cocaine, the addict is very adamant about maintaining abstinence. To the staff and other patients, however, his behavior makes no sense. My treatment staff refers to covert craving as having the *I gotta go's*. The rapid shift from involvement in treatment one day to being fixated on leaving treatment the next exemplifies the severe nature of covert craving.

The first occurrence of covert craving lasts from one to two days. It then disappears, randomly recurring to a lesser degree over the first forty-five days of recovery. If decisions are made during an episode of covert craving, the addict may find that his plans, in some subtle way, place him in jeopardy. If an addict finds himself extremely agitated and restless from time to time and feels a sense of immediacy about nonrecovery goals, it is best to stop and question whether or not this is covert craving. During treatment, *everything* else needs to become secondary to recovery.

Several rules about covert craving are:

1. Covert craving begins as overt craving disappears.

2. Covert craving is never recognized by the person experiencing it.

3. If an addict does not acknowledge quickly that his behavior reflects covert craving, no amount of arguing will convince him otherwise.

4. Covert craving subsides in one or two days.

5. A feeling of *being cured* from cocaine addiction is the best indicator of covert craving.

These rules can help an addict learn how to manage covert craving. The first skill is to anticipate covert craving as the overt craving and cocaine dreams subside. I encourage patients not to make any decisions about treatment in a period of less than two days. This will permit a return to a noncraving state before executing treatment decisions. In addition, addicts early in treatment cannot trust their own judgment. An addict may be a terrific businessman, scientist, or cook but, if he is early in treatment for cocaine dependency, his judgment about *himself* is misguided at best. Throughout recovery, but especially during the time of covert craving, an addict can learn more about himself by observing his behavior rather than analyzing his thoughts. In early recovery, an addict's thoughts are distorted by his disease, but his behavior continues to provide clues about his true feelings.

Conditioned-Cue Craving

The fourth type of craving is called *conditioned-cue craving*. Conditioned cues are produced by the learning that occurs during a cocaine binge.

Prior to each binge, an addict in Stage V experiences intense anticipation about the upcoming cocaine high. Anticipation signals the brain: pay attention, something important is about to happen. Anticipation arouses the brain and increases awareness. The high level of arousal trains the brain to expect a known event, such as a meal or sex. During this alert state, the brain takes in as much information as it can. The mind begins processing the cocaine event, asking, "Why do I feel so good?" and "Why do I feel a sense of reward?" Because cocaine has bypassed all of the conventional reward-producing behaviors, the brain cannot attribute this sense of reward to any understandable reward producing behavior. The brain then attaches meaning to more minor events and thoughts that surround the use of cocaine, thinking that these events or thoughts *must* be the reasons for such a reward.

The learning that occurs during cocaine use produces the cues that later trigger cocaine craving. The effect of this learning during the first few cocaine encounters is so intense that a cocaine addict will remember his first cocaine experiences for the rest of his life.

If these same events or thoughts recur when the addict is away from cocaine, they produce the same learned anticipation and physiologic response that occurred during the cocaine high. The anticipation drives the addict to seek cocaine. The learning about cocaine use is initially specific. During a binge, however, it generalizes into the environmental setting. If the cocaine addict was listening to a certain musical piece during a binge, he would immediately and, more importantly, forever learn to associate this musical piece with cocaine use. His mind is tricked into believing that this particular music is somehow related to cocaine euphoria. Conditioned cues are seemingly unrelated phenomena that occur on the periphery of a cocaine binge and then become associated with cocaine euphoria.

The generalized learning that occurs around cocaine use creates unusual associations. A person, an object, a setting, or a song becomes associated with euphoria and reward. If tripped, these triggers will repeatedly induce cocaine craving. These triggers are deeply imprinted in the mind and can be only mildly suppressed by conscious control. They remain intact until they are actively extinguished by behavioral conditioning.

Conditioned-cue craving begins two weeks after the addict's last cocaine use. Each episode feels overwhelming, but it need not remain that way. A major milestone of recovery occurs when the addict experiences a craving, allows it to grow, and learns to sit and watch it disappear *without using*. The repeated exposure to cocaine cravings without drug use will eliminate the sensation of inevitable cocaine use that occurs during a craving episode.

In *The Cocaine Recovery Workbook*, the addict is asked to differentiate between four types of conditioned cues:

1. **Unavoidable cues.** Triggers the addict cannot avoid even while in treatment. Examples include hearing the word *Coke* when referring to the soft drink, or seeing someone flick a butane lighter similar to one that was used to smoke crack.

2. **Cues that can be temporarily avoided, but need to be extinguished later in recovery.** These include passing through a neighborhood where one has used, or returning home if the addict used at home. Another example is seeing a quantity of cocaine on television or in a movie.

3. **Avoidable cues that are best managed by avoiding the triggering element.** An example of this type of cue is listening to the same music that one played while using. A second example is having cocaine paraphernalia around a recovering addict.

4. **Danger cues that must be avoided at any cost.** These include seeing old friends who continue to use or deal drugs or being exposed to a pile of cocaine.

Once an addict's cues have been divided into these four categories, he can develop a plan to handle each of them. Unavoidable cues are examined from day one. The power in these cues is decreased by systematic exposure. For example, the addict may need to say the word *Coke* four times an hour for five days, and note that the drug craving induced by this word decreases each day. He may need to remember certain bad feelings he had during a cocaine binge five times daily, and learn that each time he thinks about them, his cravings seem less intense.

Avoidable cues that will invariably be tripped later are best managed by using a behavioral technique known as *extinguishing*. Extinguishing treatment occurs when the addict repeatedly exposes himself to each cue (except danger cues). The addict's brain actively learns that cocaine use does not follow exposure to these triggers. This exposure eliminates the addict's response to the conditioned cue. Occasionally, a cue feels so uncomfortable that it must be eliminated through indirect exposure.[4]

Some easily avoidable cues such as specific record albums are best treated by eliminating one's exposure to them—e.g. throwing the records away. Addicts must throw out equipment that was used to administer cocaine; this paraphernalia never serves any other useful purpose. Many recovering addicts find their homes contain many cues. If they are unable to extinguish all the triggers that are generated by their home, it is best to move.

A fourth type of conditioned cue, the danger cue, needs to be avoided at all cost. These cues serve the recovering addict no benefit. Some examples of danger cues are:

- Using other drugs the addict used with cocaine.
- Being directly exposed to cocaine.
- Hanging around drug dealers.
- Engaging in *compulsive* sexual activity.
- Selling cocaine.

The addict should not expose himself to these direct threats to his sobriety. Repeated exposure to danger cues may extinguish craving, but will more likely lead to relapse.

---

4. The most effective type of indirect exposure occurs through the use of hypnosis. In a light hypnotic state, the addict is asked to experience a specific conditioned cue. This is repeated, often many times, to flood the addict with the cue until it detaches from its cocaine-related significance. This type of flooding can be done in individual therapy or even in a treatment group.

SIX

Thought Distortion

Principles

1. Cocaine distorts our animal instincts for survival.

2. Cocaine addiction contorts an addict's thinking; the most prevalent cocaine-induced distortion is denial.

3. Cocaine feels more powerful than other addictive drugs. This leads the addict to concentrate on stopping cocaine, ignoring the other components of his or her addictive disease.

4. Cocaine leaves thoughts of grandiosity in the mind long after an addict stops using.

5. Their ability to stay off cocaine during treatment deceives many addicts into thinking that life-long abstinence will be simple.

6. Addicts experience *euphoric recall* which, if left unchecked, leads to cocaine romancing and relapse.

Cocaine has many effects on the brain. In this chapter, we will learn how cocaine alters or distorts thinking. Cocaine does not modify one's concrete thoughts; it does, however, cause cognitive distortions. Addicts do not, for example, believe the world is flat; instead, they experience subtle distortions and misrepresentations about their own reality. An addict can only begin correcting the distortions when he learns that they exist.

Changes in Instincts

Principle 1 — Cocaine distorts our animal instincts for survival.

All of us have primitive drives or instincts. Our instincts are controlled in a part of our brain we inherited from our evolutionary predecessors. Instincts prevent us from starving to death or dying of dehydration. They route us away from life threatening or painful situations, and drive us to procreate. Instincts are stronger than our conscious thoughts. As humans, we sense these instincts as an impulse or need. When we act on these instincts, we feel reward. Reward reinforces the instinctive behavior. Throughout our lives we feel instinctual drives; when we properly respond to these drives our instinctual brain produces a reward.

Chapters Three and Four described how cocaine short circuits our brain's reward system. Instead of our instincts driving us to seek shelter, procure food, and then feel the rewards of these efforts, cocaine bypasses the behaviors that produce physiologic rewards and directly stimulates the reward center of the brain. This direct stimulation produces three effects:

1. Cocaine urges mimic instincts, producing a pressure or need followed by a reward during initial cocaine use.

2. Cocaine overpowers our conventional instincts, making them seem less important, or

3. Cocaine use turns our instinctual drives into bizarre rituals.

Cocaine addicts describe their cravings as intense and unavoidable urges. They believe the only way to stop the unrelenting urges is to use cocaine. Most addicts tell me that cravings are stronger than their ability to resist them. Cravings create ritualistic drug seeking that makes drug use seem inevitable. Cocaine addicts say: "I might as well give up and use now, because I know I will give in to this craving sooner or later." If the addict then begins to fantasize about using cocaine, he or she is caught in a crescendo of anticipation. The anticipation is followed by the temporary release found in drug use. This anticipation followed by release makes the cocaine ritual feel all the more like an instinctual drive.

As human beings we have several natural instinctual drives: a need to eat when hungry and drink when thirsty, a fight or flight reaction in times of danger, a sexual drive to procreate and continue our species, and a drive to avoid pain. Cocaine short circuits these instincts for self-preservation. When our instinctual center is directly and relentlessly flogged by cocaine, our normal instinctual drives are overwhelmed. Our *hunger* is stopped, often resulting in weight loss.[5] Our *fight or flight reaction* is constantly stimulated by the drug, keeping the addict from recognizing danger when he is in trouble. Many addicts have exposed themselves to extreme danger to obtain cocaine, and fail to see their activities as life threatening. Addicts consume huge quantities of cocaine, experience chest pain, heart attacks, or seizures and continue to deny that their drug use is life threatening. Cocaine distorts the *sexual drive*. During the cocaine high, many addicts experience compulsive and bizarre sexual feelings. This leads them to engage in sexual rituals they would never consider when sober. Normal sexuality is then suppressed following a binge. This stimulation, followed by repression of our sexual selves, creates significant problems in the first two years of recovery.[6] *Pain avoidance* is disrupted as well. The cocaine addict will endure the pain and suffering created as side effects of the drug in the hopes of producing cocaine euphoria. Addicts tolerate seizures, chest pain, and puncture wounds that turn into painful scars as they chase the high produced by the drug.

---

5. Some addicts who also have eating disorders welcome this appetite suppression.

6. The combination of an excitation and distortion of one's sexual drive, followed by drive suppression after a cocaine and sex binge promotes behaviors that may blossom into sexual addiction. See Chapter 10 and the work of Patrick Carnes for more information. (also see *Additional Readings*)

This disruption of human instinctual drives causes problems well into recovery. The recovering addict often makes incorrect decisions because his instincts are insufficient to direct him toward a healthy life. The instinctual brain has become toxic with chronic cocaine use. Instincts guide us in many subtle ways to make the best possible decisions about our lives. The toxic brain makes distorted decisions that feel instinctually correct because it has been corrupted by cocaine. Therefore, addicts in early recovery should not make decisions on their own. Recovering addicts should use a treatment group, their physician or counselor, or an A.A. or C.A. sponsor as a resource to assist in all major decisions. After a period of time, usually about a year, most recovering addicts are able to trust their instincts once again.

Early in recovery an addict often feels as if his life is dull or flat. He has few goals, few things that give his life meaning. This dullness or flatness develops as a result of cocaine short-circuiting the mind's instincts. Detoxification medications help in the biochemical reconstruction of the instinctual brain. However, only time will heal the wounds created by cocaine. During the waiting period, addicts must subsist on their intellect.

The Cocaine Recovery Workbook examines how each of the addict's instincts have been damaged. The workbook helps the addict take stock of excessive behaviors and instinctual deficiencies that developed as a result of cocaine. Then, with the help of treatment and twelve-step recovery groups, he must search for the path of recovery.

Denial of Cocaine Addiction

Principle 2 — Cocaine addiction contorts an addict's thinking; the most prevalent cocaine-induced distortion is denial.

The first symptom of any addictive illness is denial. Being *in denial* does not simply mean one disagrees with the statement: "I am an addict." Denial is much more complicated. Denial is composed of a series of contorted behaviors and rationalizations that permit the addict to continue using drugs and alcohol. Addicts develop rationalizations to protect and defend their addiction. It is normal for the addict to have denial about his addiction prior to treatment.

I advise patients to view their denial as a defense mechanism. Defense mechanisms protect us from the painful truth about ourselves. The truth about drug addiction is that it fills one's life with discomfort and pain. Denial protects the addict from seeing the pain caused by his cocaine addiction. Unfortunately, this only insures that the addict will continue his cocaine use.

When an addict enters treatment, the first task is to identify his denial. The addict must then examine, one by one, each of the denial mechanisms in his vast collection. If left unchecked, denial mechanisms talk one right back into using! Some common denial statements are:

- *"I just do cocaine when I need escape; I'm not addicted."* Almost every addict uses cocaine in an episodic or even sporadic manner. Cocaine users watch pill addicts, alcoholics, and narcotic addicts use every day and think: "Now *that* is being addicted. I'm glad I don't need to use like that." If an addict in treatment has these feelings, he or she should reread Chapter Three on the Cocaine Addiction Cycle, or confirm his own addiction cycle using the accompanying workbook.

- *"If you straighten out my emotional problems, I won't have a reason to use cocaine. If I have no reason to use, I'll just stop."* Addicts often believe that their emotional problems established their cocaine addiction. Many people arrive in treatment with problems in their lives that predate their cocaine use. As long as an addict holds these problems as causative for his cocaine use, he or she will be unable to stop using. When the addict stops blaming his emotional problems for his drug use, he will claim his denial and move into recovery. Then, and only then, can the addict begin healing the scars of earlier trauma.

- *"I can quit anytime. I have stopped many times in the past and I can do it again."* All addicts use for a bit, stop, and then return to another cocaine binge. Being addicted to cocaine is defined as binge use, followed by crash, feeling cured, and returning to use later on. This describes the addict caught in the Cocaine Addiction Cycle. The addict may have "stopped using" and feel freed from his cocaine habit, when in truth he is in a holding pattern, awaiting the move to Stage V (see Figure 3 in Chapter Three for a description of the Cocaine Addiction Cycle). I have yet to treat a cocaine addict that did not stop using at least once!

- *"When the seizures get bad enough, I will quit using."* Cocaine omnipotence makes addicts feel as if all of the major medical, psychiatric, and social complications of cocaine addiction just won't happen to them. They rationalize their medical complications as temporary or insignificant despite all evidence to the contrary. This type of denial is known as minimization. Cocaine addicts say they use "a little bit" and mean five grams a day. They say "I have never felt better" and in the next breath describe how every time they use they experience chest pains, a sign of heart disease. The workbook exercises for Chapter Two will help the addict quantify the damage caused by cocaine. When an addict hears other addicts' stories and looks for the similarities in himself, he will stop minimizing the effects that cocaine had on his life.

- *"I have great insight into other people's problems, so I must understand myself as well."* Cocaine creates a subtle but pervasive distortion in self-awareness. This complex distortion fools the addict into thinking he has his own best interests at heart. Patients who are cocaine dependent often provide excellent feedback to others about their problems. This makes them believe that their thinking about themselves is accurate as well. However, the cocaine rattled brain produces an unusual twist. The toxic addict is frequently well aware of outside situations, but exhibits poor judgment about his or her own life. Constant confrontation concerning these judgments helps the addict learn to listen to others and assimilate their advice.

- *"I feel fine about myself and my life. It's just that from time to time I go on a long cocaine binge."* Cocaine denial is different from the denial seen in alcohol addiction. The cocaine addict experiences the physical and psychic trauma of a binge as an isolated event—his withdrawal symptoms seem negligible and short-lived. The addict sees himself as walking down a merry lane, from time to time inexplicably stumbling into the snake pit of a cocaine binge. He lacks perspective and cannot see his entire life going downhill because of his addiction.

- *"If you had my set of problems you would use cocaine too."* This type of denial is often called "the poor pitiful me's." It is uncommon among cocaine addicts. It occurs more often in alcohol or polydrug addicts. When it does occur, however, the addict uses cocaine in a whirlwind of self-destructive binges. Hoping to get away from his troubles, this type of addict only magnifies his problems. Cocaine use solves nothing, and any problem is only made worse by cocaine use. From time to time a cocaine addict will tell me that he uses cocaine because he has money problems. I usually remark: "Well, I'm sure you fixed your money problems by spending it all on cocaine!"

During treatment, each rationalization about cocaine use must be systematically examined. In *The Cocaine Recovery Workbook*, the addict is asked to write down each of these rationalizations for using cocaine. Remember, these thoughts never *seem* like justifications. However, when they are discussed in a group setting—preferably with other cocaine addicts—the denial intrinsic in these rationalizations will be confronted, and the truth will emerge. When the addict truly sees his rationalizations for what they are and becomes committed to changing them, the process of recovery can begin.

Denial can linger for months and even years into recovery. During treatment it is more important to notice each instance of denial than to try to eliminate it completely. Denial is a normal part of recovery, not a sign of failed treatment. Once an addict exhibits *denial thinking*, he should label it as such. Then, the addict should explore what the thought pushes him to do. He must not act on denial thoughts, only notice them. When in treatment, addicts are initially ashamed of denial thoughts. These thoughts are normal, neither good nor bad. The addict should write these thoughts down, and share them with someone else. When he trains himself to go through this exercise with each thought of denial, the level of his denial drops automatically.

The addict also addresses his denial when he works a twelve-step recovery program. Each of the Twelve Steps helps the addict, in various ways, recover from his addiction. The major task of the first step is to help the addict admit that he has an addiction problem. The next two steps of the twelve-step program continue to focus the addict on his denial.

Denial of Other Facets of Addiction

Principle 3 — Cocaine feels more powerful than other addictive drugs. This leads the addict to concentrate on stopping cocaine, ignoring the other components of his or her addictive disease.

Addiction is a problem inside people, not a characteristic of a white powder. Some people appear to be prone to develop addictive disease. If these genetically or environmentally susceptible people use cocaine, their use turns into addiction very quickly. If these same susceptible people were to use other drugs or alcohol, they would be just as likely to develop an addictive illness—albeit at a slower pace. Cocaine addiction develops faster than any other type of addiction. As a result, addicts feel so overwhelmed by cocaine, that their more insidious addictive behaviors seem distant from the cocaine crisis at hand.

An addict who first used cocaine may start drinking to modulate the unpleasant side effects of the cocaine high. Conversely, an addict may have begun his addiction with a significant dependency on alcohol, marijuana, nicotine, or other drugs and then moved on to using cocaine. Either way, many addicts become dependent on more than one drug. *The Cocaine Recovery Workbook* directs the addict to review his drug and alcohol use, dividing it into three categories. These are:

1. Modulator drug use to temper the unpleasant cocaine side effects during Stages I-III.

2. Second choice drugs: drugs that cocaine addicts use when they can not procure their drug of choice.

3. Other drugs and behaviors that are already addictions in and of themselves.

Once the addict defines his relationship with drugs other than cocaine, he should work on the denial that keeps him from owning his addiction to each substance. A user may have residual doubts about giving up all their addictive drugs at once. Addicts say: "But I came here to stop cocaine, not to deal with these other things!" People with addictive disease display the most denial about their deepest addictions. If an addict finds himself staunchly defending his right to drink alcohol or smoke cigarettes after giving up cocaine, he has the deepest attachment to these substances, not to cocaine!

Many cocaine addicts have eating disorders, problems with compulsive sexual behaviors, gambling, or shoplifting. Each of these addictive behaviors is part of the entire addictive syndrome, they do not occur in a vacuum. Often an addict will abuse other drugs or alcohol, or engage in compulsive behaviors while he uses cocaine. He begins to pair cocaine with other drugs or behaviors that comprise his addictive syndrome. The paired euphoria is greater than the sum of both addictive parts. This pairing increases the addict's likelihood of a relapse into cocaine use if he does not discontinue the other components of his addiction. The majority of relapses in cocaine addicted patients are triggered by using alcohol or other modulator drugs, or engaging in paired addictive behaviors. Using alcohol also decreases an addict's resistance to the intense cravings encountered in Stage V, giving the addict permission to embark on cocaine seeking behavior, and subsequent relapse.

As addicts move further into recovery, they are able to see past their denial mechanisms. Within the first two months of a drug-free recovery, most addicts accept that their use of other drugs or alcohol is part of their addictive disease. Later, cocaine addicts learn to see their compulsive sexuality, their nicotine use, their eating disorder, or their gambling as facets of one problem—addictive disease.

Grandiosity

Principle 4 — Cocaine leaves thoughts of grandiosity in the mind long after an addict stops using.

When first under the influence of cocaine, the user feels powerful, even invincible. Cocaine makes the user feel smart, clear headed, and strong. But when the user runs out of cocaine, and progresses to the cocaine crash, much of the cocaine effect disappears. However, the sense of invincibility lingers on: the addict feels he is impervious to cocaine. If he deals cocaine to support his habit, the addict feels he will never get caught. Many cocaine addicts imagine themselves outsmarting the world, and feel as if their habit is a well-guarded secret.

When such an addict arrives in treatment, he has feelings of omnipotence. "This treatment stuff does not look hard!" he says quietly to himself. Grandiosity keeps the addict from seeing the calamity of his situation. He feels different from others. The supposed difference arises from a sense of omnipotence, or its alter ego, low self-esteem.

Not all addicts suffer from residual grandiosity when they arrive in treatment. Some addicts feel completely overwhelmed and immobilized by their life situation. However, when they begin to feel better, they quickly move past a reasonable understanding of themselves and join other cocaine addicts in their grandiose thinking. This oscillation between feeling devastated and invincible is characteristic of the cocaine addict. The oscillation mirrors the switch in mood from cocaine use in Stage I to cocaine crash in Stage II of the Cocaine Addiction Cycle.

Grandiose feelings linger for the first several months of recovery. They need to be tempered with the voice of reason. *The Cocaine Recovery Workbook* describes several exercises that work to diminish grandiose thoughts when they occur. Like thoughts of denial, these grandiose thoughts should be shared with others. Often in the telling they are tempered or tamed.

False Confidence

Principle 5 — Their ability to stay off cocaine during treatment deceives many addicts into thinking that life-long abstinence will be simple.

When an addict is hospitalized for cocaine dependency, initially he experiences a feeling of relief; he is physically removed from his cocaine source. This sense of relief often leads to a false confidence: "I've had no cravings for the past six weeks, so I think I will have no problems with sobriety when I leave." He finds it easy to remain off of cocaine while in treatment. Soon, this false sense of security, when combined with unrecognized or covert drug craving, makes the addict feel that continued treatment is no longer necessary. He reenters his old environment, and is exposed to all of the old cocaine cues. If the addict has no place to process his craving, these cues can lead the self-sure addict into relapse.

Individuals feel as if they are cured very early on in cocaine addiction treatment, and often leave full of energy about their new life. This excitement is often crushed by reality. Therefore, a gradually increasing exposure to the outside world is often best. With each added exposure, if the addict avoids using, he decreases the probability of relapse. Chapter Nine of this book guides cocaine addicts through the progressive exposure necessary for cocaine recovery.

The majority of relapses following treatment occur because of these three factors: relief that cravings have dissipated, combined with residual grandiosity, followed by exposure to a previously conditioned cue.

The most effective form of treatment for cocaine dependency lasts at least a year.[7] A year-long treatment program should contain most of these four elements:

1. Initial inpatient or residential treatment that removes the addict from his using environment for two to eight weeks, followed by

2. Increasing exposure to the outside world through a return to work *or* home while attending a partial day treatment or remaining in a residential treatment setting.

3. Twice weekly group therapy along with daily twelve-step meeting attendance. During this phase, random drug screens may help keep the addict from taking the first drink or drug.

4. Twelve-step meeting attendance should continue to be an integral part of a recovering addict's life. This will prevent the addict from drifting back to any of the many addictive behaviors that were identified during the treatment process.

Euphoric Recall

Principle 6 — Addicts experience *euphoric recall* which, if left unchecked, leads to cocaine romancing and relapse.

Previously, the reader learned that early cocaine use produces a memory of euphoria deep inside the feeling brain. The

---

7. Treatment for cocaine addiction is not inexpensive. Many insurance carriers, frustrated by the poor recovery rate for cocaine addiction and the rising cost of medical care, have decreased benefits at a time when many addicts need it most. Low-cost treatment is available through state and county agencies in most parts of the United States.

memory is very intense, as cocaine directly stimulates the brain's reward center. The memory is also ill-formed, as the brain cannot attribute the reward to any known, natural, reward-producing event.

As his addiction progresses, an addict develops more and more problems with cocaine and the cocaine high grows less euphoric. The binges become filled with paranoia, depression, agitation, and an escalating drive to use more and more cocaine. The addict enjoys cocaine less each time and the cocaine crash produces increasing despondency. Each of these uncomfortable memories is stored in the mind, overshadowed by the euphoric memories.

Almost every addict arrives in treatment filled with remorse for what he has done to his spouse, parents, children, coworkers, and family. He feels desperate about the financial, social, legal, and health consequences of his addiction. He may feel empty and depressed about how he has let himself and everyone else down. However, when asked about what the cocaine high was like, he drops his hang-dog expression, and his eyes light up. He describes how great cocaine made him feel. He feels euphoric remembering the cocaine high, and the tragic consequences are forgotten. The complications he suffered from cocaine use are completely disconnected from his memory of the cocaine high. This is *euphoric recall*. Euphoric recall is a property of the brain peculiar to addicts. It consists of the ability to reexperience all of the good feelings associated with cocaine use *without* a memory connection to the devastating consequences that were directly linked to the cocaine high.

Euphoric recall does not signify that a person's recovery is in jeopardy. Many recovering addicts come to me and cautiously say, "There is a part of me that still wants to use cocaine." They are often afraid to discuss these thoughts with anyone in treatment. They are worried that they will be judged poorly because they still have positive thoughts about using cocaine. They wonder if there is something wrong with them. After talking for a time, it becomes obvious that they are suffering from euphoric recall of past cocaine use.

From time to time, every addict experiences euphoric recall. Euphoric recall cannot be eliminated. The addict can, however, compensate for its existence. If the addict continues to think or talk about his pleasant cocaine escapades he prolongs the recall and begins *drug romancing*. Drug romancing and cocaine craving are the products of euphoric recall. The addict has to train himself to manage euphoric recall so that it does not become drug craving or drug romancing.

When an addict finds himself experiencing euphoric recall, he should simply label it as such. If the recall then progresses to drug romancing (in his head or in conversation with others), he can take any of these steps:

- **Thought stopping.** When drug romancing begins, the addict talks to himself, telling himself to stop thinking about cocaine.

- **Thought substitution.** The addict can interrupt his drug romancing by switching his train of thought to something else. This requires a conscious effort, such as thinking: "I must stop these thoughts, so I will now think about ...." He consciously strives to keep his mind on the new subject until the pressure created by euphoric recall dissipates. This usually takes five to thirty minutes. Addicts often find that it helps to move themselves physically to another chair in the room or to go outside when they practice thought substitution.

- **Forced memory connections.** When drug romancing begins, the addict forces his mind to review the consequences of his worst cocaine nightmare. By forcing his mind to connect the traumas created by cocaine use to euphoric recall, the addict is building memory bridges that his mind has failed to develop on its own. This conscious exercise needs to be repeated over and over again to be effective. This mental exercise is illustrated in *The Cocaine Recovery Workbook*.

Above all else, the addict must not berate himself for having euphoric recall. Euphoric recall is a badge of recovery. When an addict experiences euphoric recall, he should let it play out briefly, note that it is a clear reminder that he is a cocaine addict, and move onto other activities. When euphoric recall occurs in treatment, it is a golden opportunity to work on recovery skills. The addict should discuss this feeling with the treatment staff, and practice thought stopping, thought substitution, or forced memory connections. When he learns to manage his euphoric recall, the addict can live without the fear of cocaine thoughts progressing to cocaine use.

Euphoric recall diminishes over time but never completely disappears. Addicts with ten years of recovery still have memories of cocaine use touched with euphoric recall. In long-term recovery, cocaine addicts become less impressed with their episodes of euphoric recall, learning to switch them off quickly. In early recovery, euphoric recall can be frightening; in long-term recovery, it is just annoying.

SEVEN

Mood Problems

Principles

1. Cocaine addicts experience predictable mood fluctuations during the first seven to eleven days of abstinence.

2. Cocaine use generates periods of wide mood swings.

3. Cocaine use produces depression.

4. Chronic drug and alcohol use disconnects the addict from his or her feelings.

In this chapter, I will examine how cocaine affects a person's moods. Emotions such as sadness, depression, happiness, and elation all come from the feeling brain. Our moods and emotions are modulators of our experience. If we feel happy when we perform a particular task, it changes how we feel about that task. Sometimes we are aware of our moods; at other times we may not be. Whether or not we recognize our mood, it continues to color our experience of reality. Needless to say, our moods are profoundly affected by cocaine.

We develop tolerance to our moods. Repeated exposure to the same experience produces less and less of a realization of the mood that a particular experiences generates. For example, human beings rapidly habituate to cocaine euphoria, so that after repeated use the cocaine euphoria is less intense. Similarly, the addict becomes inured to his cocaine-induced depression. If he experiences depression over a period of time, his sensitivity and insight about how depressed he has become will decrease. Addicts learn to tolerate or dismiss the depths of cocaine crash depression. When they enter treatment, most people sense that something is wrong, but appear to be completely unaware that they are depressed.

Cocaine addiction creates an effect opposite from what is intended. Wishing to feel happy, the addict winds up depressed. Wishing to feel better about his life, he feels worse. Hoping to have a consistent outlook on his life, his moods became erratic and unpredictable. Depression and mood instability are the two major consequences of cocaine use. These consequences appear at predictable points on the road to recovery.

The First Week of Abstinence

Principle 1 — Cocaine addicts experience predictable mood fluctuations during the first seven to eleven days of abstinence.

When a person first uses cocaine, one of the rewards that drives him to repeated use is the cocaine-induced euphoria. No one uses cocaine to feel depressed, yet repeated use always produces periods of depression. Addicts describe paradoxical dysphoria after consuming cocaine (Stage I). Paradoxical dysphoria occurs when, right at the point of the drug entering the body, the addict feels intensely despondent instead of euphoric. Most addicts also develop deeper depressions following a binge (in Stage III of the Cocaine Addiction Cycle).

When addicts arrive in treatment they feel quite despondent about their future. Remorse and embarrassment are common. Add shame to this state of affairs, and depression deepens further. Some addicts feel suicidal, a state created by the overwhelming despair with which they view their circumstances, combined with the depressant effects of cocaine on the brain.

Mood Problems

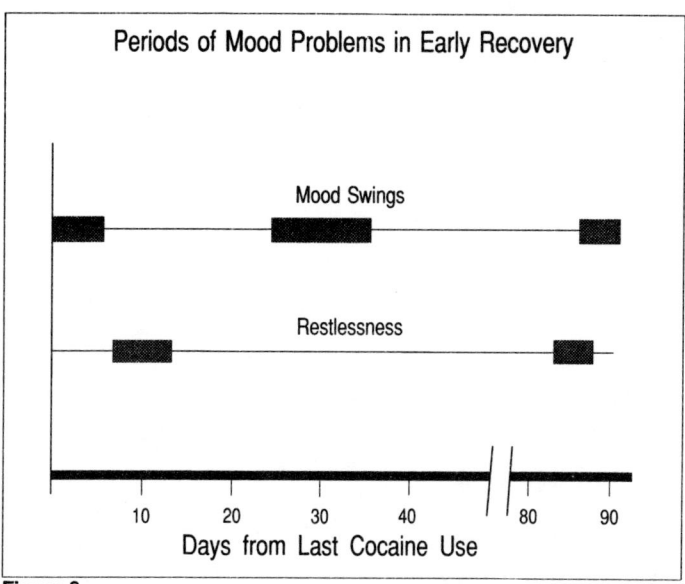

Figure 8
Cocaine addicts often suffer from intense mood swings during early recovery. The boxes above indicate common periods of mood swings and restlessness.

This period of deep depression lasts for twenty-four to forty-eight hours, and then begins to improve (see Figure 8). Little need be done except to wait for this initial depression to lift. After the first three to five days, it seems to improve dramatically.

When the addict reaches the first three to five days of abstinence, the initial depression lifts and he finds himself more hopeful. This plateau period lasts only a brief period of time, commonly five to seven days. During this time, patients should try to address the major catastrophes that prompted their admission into treatment. They should call work and family, and attempt to place on hold their major financial and legal problems. Cocaine addicts have a tendency to try to correct everything during this time; this is impossible. Therefore,

I recommend placing life problems in a priority order, and addressing only the most threatening. Once these calls have been made, the addict is ready for treatment and the rocky, but rewarding, times ahead.

Principle 2 — Cocaine use generates periods of wide mood swings.

One week after discontinuing cocaine, most addicts experience a time of erratic mood swings from content and happy to tense and discontent. Their fluctuating emotions cause them to feel as if they are tied to a roller coaster. During this period of mood swings, many people drop out of treatment and relapse into cocaine use. During this time, the addict believes his feelings are coming from the events around him, but they are not. The mood swings are generated by the brain. Used to cyclic cocaine use, the brain creates a cycle of unrest that the addict perceives as a period of erratic feelings. This period of mood swings corresponds to the peak period of covert craving (see Chapter Five), making the addict doubly at risk.

The emotional roller coaster ride lasts two to three days. During this time, the newly recovering addict may run to his counselor or physician and tell them that he intends to discontinue treatment, divorce his wife, quit his job, or move to Mexico. No outside decisions should be made during this time, as the addict will regret all of them. Moods will even out after the first seven to eleven days of abstinence. The period of violent mood swings has completed its course.

The pink cloud

After the intense mood swings of early treatment, most people have one additional period of mood abnormality. This period is called the *pink cloud*. Not all cocaine addicted patients experience the pink cloud. Indeed, it occurs more frequently in patients who are recovering from alcohol, sedatives, or narcotics. The pink cloud period does not start until after two weeks of abstinence. It may not begin for up to two months of abstinence. The pink cloud lasts from one week to one month in most recovering people.

The pink cloud is a period of peace, low anxiety, and somewhat unrealistic expectations about one's future. No one knows why it occurs. It may be created by the *survivor syndrome;* people who have undergone an extremely traumatic period in their lives are often so excited about being alive that they become euphoric. The addict in early recovery is like a holocaust survivor—overjoyed, and incredulous that he is alive. I instruct addicts to ride out the pink cloud but, more importantly, to enjoy it! Due to a grand, exaggerated sense of optimism, the addict should avoid making life long plans. An addict's optimism during this period may stimulate unrealistic expectations about the future. Unfortunately, reality will soon seep into the addict's consciousness, pushing out the pink cloud.

Cocaine-Induced Depression

Principle 3 — Cocaine use produces depression.

After the initial cocaine crash and the time of mood swings, addicts in recovery are left in a baseline state. In this state, most cocaine addicts feel a mild flatness or dysphoria for the first six to nine months of recovery (with the exception of the pink cloud period mentioned above). This flat sensation is a form of anhedonic depression, induced by chronic cocaine consumption. Anhedonia occurs when the primitive (hedonic) pleasures have been short circuited by continued cocaine use. Addicts experience anhedonia as a loss of enthusiasm for their hobbies, friends, family, or job.

Why does cocaine use produce anhedonia? As described in Chapter Four, cocaine produces the sensation of reward by flooding the reward center in the brain. Once flooded, the reward center fatigues, and conventional rewards feel less intense. Cocaine use depletes crucial neurotransmitters that are necessary to create the experience of reward and happiness. The neurotransmitter depletion generates the anhedonic state. Cocaine-induced anhedonic depression is a true biochemical depression, lasting for six to nine months after the last use of cocaine.

On occasion, anhedonic depression can be quite severe. It may be accompanied by other depression symptoms such as sleep problems, appetite problems, a generalized blue feeling, and even thoughts of suicide. All this is produced by the toxic effects of cocaine on a susceptible brain. I recommend that recovering people consider antidepressant medication only if the severity of depression interferes with important activities. Although an addict may experience a severe depression in the first six months of recovery, this does not mean he will be depressed for the rest of his life. If a patient feels his depression is severe and it has never been addressed, he should talk with his treatment team or physician. The addict must not make decisions about his mood on his own, as this usually results in disaster.

Affect-Oriented Psychotherapy

Principle 4 — Chronic drug and alcohol use disconnects the addict from his or her feelings.

For a long time, a central element in the treatment of chemical dependency has been a type of psychotherapy that focuses on learning to experience and understand one's feelings. Unresolved or repressed feelings about past events cause distress and often fuel a relapse into cocaine addiction. Repressed past emotional trauma prevents the recovery reflex from occurring. For these reasons, learning how to handle loss, anger, fear, sadness, and loneliness is critical for recovery. In treatment, each problem emotion is handled in a different manner.

Grief

Many addicts arrive in treatment with unresolved grief. The normal process of grieving is blocked when an addict consumes drugs or alcohol. An addict who was using around the time of a major life crisis has completely disrupted his or her normal grief response. If the cocaine user loses a loved one,

Mood Problems

loses custody of children, gets divorced, or has other losses while using or in early recovery, he will be unable to work through the grief process. This prevents the addict from resolving his grief, holding him in a fixed, raw place of constant pain.

When an addict stops his addictive behaviors, it seems as if all of his grief from the past comes forward to haunt him. I encourage addicts to approach these losses head on. Treatment is a time of support, and everyone needs support to feel grief. The addict should compile a list of losses and make a commitment to look at each loss in therapy. Addicts need not experience all grief issues at once. In fact, grief work is best handled slowly and systematically. The treatment team counsels the addict to pace himself—to disclose, discuss, and discharge the anger, loneliness, and pain about each loss in a group or individual psychotherapy setting.

One major loss that every addict must address is the loss of his best friend, cocaine. It is normal to have grief over the loss of cocaine and other chemicals. Many addicts need to write a *Dear John letter* to their long time companions, drugs and alcohol. This too is best processed in a group psychotherapy setting while in treatment.

What happens if an addict does not deal with his grief? First, he remains stuck in a painful place, making recovery more painful than using. Second, unresolved grief is a trigger to relapse into chemical dependency.

Anger

Anger is a difficult emotion for human beings, especially addicts. Most addicts suppress, misdirect, or mislabel their anger. Many addicts spend their lives trying not to feel angry. Cocaine addicts have problems expressing anger from the past, especially toward their parents or parental figures. If anger is not properly exposed and metabolized, it turns inward, creating depression or resentment. As a group, addicts are prone to develop resentments. In treatment, cocaine addicts spend much of their therapy time uncovering their resentments. Learning to handle resentments is central to recovery. Steps Four and Five of the twelve-step program focus on the resentments of the past.

Everyone has an anger style. Exercises in *The Cocaine Recovery Workbook* help the addict learn more about his style of handling anger. Once an addict learns about his style, he can develop a different, healthy strategy for experiencing his anger about life. He can learn to direct anger outward, and discover how to let it go. If an addict does not let go of his anger, his anger commonly becomes self-abusive. The most common form of self-abuse is relapse. The addict who is unable to discharge his anger expresses this inward directed anger through drug use and by destroying his life.

A smaller group of cocaine addicts give vent to a continuous feeling that appears on the surface to be anger but, on closer inspection, is not anger at all. Others always comment on how angry these addicts appear. This pseudo-anger masquerades as anger and, like anger, it keeps people away. It is, however, a defense against other emotions, usually feelings of hurt and abandonment. Addicts with these defenses need to learn how not to push others away with their hostilities. When they drop their pseudo-anger, they are able to learn how to handle the underlying feelings of loneliness and abandonment.

Loneliness

As a cocaine addict falls deeper and deeper into the Cocaine Addiction Cycle, he begins to withdraw from others. He moves into a state of isolation. Or he may spend time with others, but only over a pile of cocaine. He feels shame about his cocaine use and, unable to share this shame, he withdraws into himself.

Most addicts think: "No one feels as I do." This is indeed a lonely place. Entering treatment is often the first step in combating this loneliness. In treatment, the addict begins to realize that many people feel as alone as he felt during his cocaine days. Addiction-induced loneliness is treated by sharing with others the feelings of isolation that occurred during drug use, and looking for the common bond of recovery. Time and new-found friendships heal the past, but only if the addict reaches out to others.

When the addict reaches toward his peers, he feels support. With support, the addict must look back on the loneliness he felt at other times in life. The cause of this loneliness is different for each of us. Perhaps a parent was absent, abusive, or nonsupportive. Perhaps a spouse or close friend left, causing great pain. Perhaps the addict suffered physical, emotional, or sexual abuse and had no one to turn to. Each of these situations creates loneliness. Expressing this loneliness promotes healing.

In treatment feelings of loneliness are displaced by support and companionship. Treatment begins when one learns how others can help. When the addict completes treatment, he or she must continue to use the support of a sponsor and a peer group in twelve-step recovery to survive drug-free. Reaching out in treatment teaches the addict how to use the support of a recovering peer group for ongoing support in sobriety.

Sadness

Sadness is different than depression. Sadness is a feeling, while depression is a state created by sadness, loneliness, anger, and unresolved grief. Sadness is a simple emotion that can be very deep and intense. Sadness often creates tears. Many people suffer with sadness because as children they were told not to cry, or their tears were belittled. This suppressed their ability to manage their sadness, which in turn causes emotional distress and depression.

The solution to this is simple: learn to cry again. By releasing tears, we allow ourselves to release pent up feelings. Crying is simply the brain's physiological manner of releasing sadness and hurt. When a cocaine addict arrives in treatment, his feelings are often convoluted from not allowing himself to cry for many years. Early life messages, when combined with societal taboos about tears, train the addict not to let go of his sadness. In individual or group therapy, many addicts need to learn to cry again. By relearning this physiological process, a person will address sadness and lessen its deep-rooted effect. Then and only then will recovery seem easier.

Drug use suppresses the addict's feelings about everything. When an addict enters treatment, he feels anger, sadness, hurt, loneliness, and other emotions from his past. It is critical, therefore, for the addict to spend time in therapy experiencing a range of feelings. He should capture time in group therapy, individual therapy, and support groups to explore his feelings. Addicts need to vent their feelings, not manipulate, suppress, or disconnect them. When patients ask what will allow them to recover, I tell them: "Become friends with your feelings; then they will not create relapse."

EIGHT

The Twelve Steps

Principles

1. Today, most treatments for addictive illnesses are based on the twelve-step program of recovery.

2. For the first three months of recovery, the addict should concentrate his efforts on understanding steps one through three.

3. Step One directs addicts to consider that they have no control over their drug use, and that their lives are out of control.

4. Step Two directs the addict to look for a power outside himself that will help him recover.

5. Step Three pushes the addict to shift the focus of control to a higher power.

Up until now, this book has delineated techniques to help the addict become involved in treatment and stay there. The toxic effects of cocaine on the mind and body, the detoxification process, and the types of drug craving have been described. The thinking distortions and mood problems of early recovery were then illustrated. Although this information covers a lot of territory, it is only the preamble to the recovery process from cocaine addiction.

This chapter examines the question: "What is the path of recovery?" For most addicts, the path of recovery is guided by the twelve-step recovery program of Alcoholics Anonymous, Narcotics Anonymous, and Cocaine Anonymous. Twelve-step recovery is indeed a process or path. It is not an idea, a concept, or a thought about oneself. It is an attitude about life, a way of looking at things, and a belief system. Twelve-step recovery is an evolving direction, rather than a place to stand in life.

Principle 1 — Today, most treatments for addictive illnesses are based on the twelve-step program of recovery.

Treatment would not be what it is today without the recovering communities of C.A., N.A., A.A., Al-Anon, Nar-Anon, O.A., O-Anon, Codependents Anonymous, and a myriad of other twelve-step groups. All of these groups are based on the Twelve Steps of Alcoholics Anonymous. Why do most treatment centers encourage patients to follow the path of the twelve-step recovery program? Simply stated, it works. Staying off of cocaine is difficult. Left to their own devices, most addicts eventually return to drug or alcohol use. Changing this tendency takes nothing short of a new way of looking at one's life. This is what twelve-step recovery gives the addict. Daily support to change old behaviors takes a caring support group, and A.A., N.A., and C.A. offer just that.

This book is not designed to be an introduction to A.A. Many excellent introductions to the Twelve Steps of Alcoholics Anonymous are available. Treatment centers utilize written materials, twelve-step meetings, step study meetings, and readings from the "Big Book" to help patients understand the program.

As a minimum, I recommend reading the following:

- *Alcoholics Anonymous,* the A.A. "Big Book"
- *Twelve Steps and Twelve Traditions*
- *Narcotics Anonymous,* the "Blue Book."

Using the educational material in *The Cocaine Recovery Book* helps the addict along the path of recovery, but it is vitally important for everyone to read and discuss twelve-step literature. *The Cocaine Recovery Workbook* directs the addict to read and discuss pertinent sections in the above three books. It also guides addicts through programmed exercises that increase their understanding of this literature.

Principle 2 — For the first three months of recovery, the addict should concentrate his efforts on understanding steps one through three.

While in the first ninety days of recovery, I strongly suggest that the addict concentrate on understanding the first three steps of A.A. When studying the first three steps, it is normal to have reservations, doubts, or even frank skepticism about the program. If an addict has problems accepting the twelve-step philosophy, he should not panic. Struggling with the concepts of recovery is a healthy sign, a normal part of recovery. The addict needs only to be open to the changes that come from working the steps. The A.A. program creates change in many areas of an addict's life. The first change will be in how the addict views addiction and himself as an addict.

The addict should consider the steps of A.A. in sequence, starting with Step One. If a cocaine addict feels that the only addiction problem he has is with cocaine, then he should read the literature focusing on his cocaine problem. At some point, many addicts identify other chemicals and behaviors that are part of their addictive illness.

After the first ninety days of recovery, the addict can explore, at a varying pace, steps four through nine. Much of the transformation that occurs in recovery is created by the reframing of one's concept of self by the Twelve Steps of A.A.; the change created by the steps is most profound when it is not rushed. The later steps help create change in every area of the addict's life, rather than addressing directly an addict's compulsive use of drugs. Take the A.A. philosophy and approach to recovery a day at a time.

Step One

Principle 3 — Step One directs addicts to consider that they have no control over their drug use, and that their lives are out of control.

Step One reads: *We admitted we were powerless over alcohol (and other mood altering drugs)—that our lives had become unmanageable.* Step One can be broken into three distinct parts.

The first part of Step One, the admission, embodies a submission. When we do something wrong, it is best to admit this to others. Step One does not say that the addict was happy with cocaine, that he was empowered by his relationship with cocaine, or even that he had a notion that he was in a bit of a jam. Step One asks the addict to submit, to "say uncle" to his cocaine problem. It may seem strange to ask an addict to give up before he even starts recovery. However, submitting to the concept that cocaine is more powerful than you is the first step to conquering the problem.

Scientists and scholars who are unfamiliar with twelve-step recovery have problems with the concept of submission in recovery. One of the great paradoxes in recovery is that the addict gains power over his life when he gives up on his attempts to control his addiction. For some, giving up may be easy. Some addicts arrive in treatment defeated, overwhelmed, and exhausted. For these people, the admission of Step One is a statement of fact.

Others are still trying to gain some control over their lives. They do not like the thought that they have no control over anything. New members of a twelve-step group should focus on something over which they lost control because of their cocaine use. The addict must examine specifically what he can admit about his cocaine binges. Did they keep him from his family and friends? Was needed money spent on cocaine instead? Once the addict is able to admit a small part of his loss of control, the admission of powerlessness is not far behind.

The second concept in Step One is powerlessness. This too is paradoxical. How can anyone expect a person to stop using cocaine if that person has no power over drugs? Step One does not stipulate that no power exists anywhere to stop addiction. It states that *the addict* is powerless. This implies that the power to quit comes from a place outside of the addict himself.

While using, the addict was not in control, the drug had a power over him, guiding his thoughts and his actions. The central theme of Step One is the realization that the addict's life was controlled by an external force, and that force was cocaine. Even when he was not actively using, the cocaine addict was moved through the Cocaine Addiction Cycle by his cocaine habit.

As human beings, we want to feel as if we are in control of our lives. Step One does not instruct the addict to sign his life over to someone else. The powerlessness concept in Step One asserts that the addict has already done that—with cocaine. When the addict examines the Twelve Steps he will see that the next two steps offer direction toward a more benevolent controller.

While it is true that cocaine addicts are also powerless over other mood altering drugs, it is recommended that they initially take the first step for cocaine alone, all the while abstaining from other drugs and alcohol. In time, addicts see that their problem is with all mood altering drugs, not just cocaine. The addict can then take Step One with his other addictive substances and behaviors. Many compulsive feelings about alcohol, drugs, or other addictive behaviors are frequently masked by cocaine use. If the addict keeps his mind open, he will soon understand that powerlessness does not rest within the drugs themselves, but in the addict. The Twelve Steps help the addict accept that addiction is a quality of the mind. Addiction does not exist in a bottle or a gram of cocaine.

The third major component of Step One is the concept of unmanageability. Step One states: We admitted we are powerless over cocaine (and other mood altering drugs) —*that our lives had become unmanageable.* Addicts have one of two defenses against seeing the unmanageability described in Step One. One type of addict might say: "Oh, I may not have control (I'm powerless) over cocaine, but I don't see that there have been any real problems from this." The addict admits that the use of cocaine may be problematic, but denies any negative consequences from this use. This defense is infrequent with cocaine addicts, because cocaine use is very disruptive to everyday living.

A second type of addict may admit that his life is out of control and that he has problems managing his affairs.

However, he will transfer the cause of his problems onto things other than drug use, such as his marriage or his job. It is difficult for him to admit that his problems really arise from a single cause—substance abuse. After all, if he really accepted that drugs were a problem, then he would have to quit!

Every person in early recovery must examine the defenses that prevent him from admitting unmanageability. *The Cocaine Recovery Workbook* will help the addict determine if he is trying to suppress or displace his feelings of unmanageability. Each cocaine-induced change that increases unmanageability may be subtle. Each subtle change is masked from the addict's view by the toxic effects of cocaine on the brain. Therefore, with each additional problem, the addict senses little change. One day, he awakens in the morning wondering how his life has become such a mess. The slowly mounting problems, combined with a shifting cocaine attitude, created his troubles. The changes were induced by cocaine at a biochemical level, and are thus imperceptible to the addict himself. His life seems a mess, but cocaine seems to be outside the cause of his troubles. Step One points directly at cocaine addiction as being at the center of the problem.

Step One makes a crucial point about the mind of an addict. When one is addicted, it is as if there are two people inside, fighting for control. Before entering recovery, the addict inside is winning, is controlling a person's behaviors. The addict, not the person, bent decisions, values, and beliefs in many subtle ways to produce the downhill slide into addiction.

Step Two

Principle 4 — Step Two directs the addict to look for a power outside himself that will help him recover.

Step Two states: *We came to believe that a power greater than ourselves could restore us to sanity.* When the addict discerns that he is not in control of his life, he finds himself in a dilemma. If an addict early in recovery attempts to take control of his life, he cannot prevent the addict within him from creating further unmanageability. Step Two solves the dilemma: If I cannot control myself, where should the control come from? It further extends the paradox of gaining control by letting go.

The first part of Step Two states: *We came to believe....* To come to believe implies trust. It requires a faith that a higher power has your own best interest at heart and, more importantly, that you did *not* have your own best interest at heart. Step Two does not say we had a thought, or considered the possibility, or wondered if a power greater than ourselves could restore us to sanity. It states we came to believe, that we had a leap of faith, not an intellectual consideration.

The second portion of Step Two attempts to define the phrase "a power greater than yourself." Most people in western society equate a power greater than themselves with God. Step Two does not demand that one seek God. It only demands that one does not think of himself as God. The hedonistic, self-serving qualities of cocaine dependence made the addict feel as if he were the center of the universe. Step Two directly attacks this cocaine-generated grandiosity.

Most people involved in twelve-step recovery spend considerable time exploring their concept of a higher power. The search begins with the admission of personal powerlessness. Some members of twelve-step groups may rediscover the God of their youth. However, many new members are wary of organized religion. They may begin by designating their treatment providers or the group itself as their higher power. Usually, the concept of a higher power evolves over time to become a close personal relationship with a God of *one's own personal understanding*. Step Two does not dictate who one's higher power is; it simply states that the addict needs to believe in a power greater than himself. For the cocaine addict, the core of Step Two is the shifting of control away from himself and into the care of a power greater than and outside of himself.

The third section of Step Two states: ...would restore us to sanity. Implicit in this section of Step Two is the belief that cocaine and other drug addiction has driven the addict insane.

Cocaine addicts often say "I'm thinking just fine now." The notion of insanity is too hard to bear. When an addict has difficulty accepting the insanity portion of Step Two, I suggest that he write down some of the things he has done to obtain cocaine and some of the excuses that he used to justify the money he spent on the drug. These exercises are in *The Cocaine Recovery Workbook*. When he has completed this, the addict should ask himself if his behavior does not seem insane.

Many addicts say "Well, I did those things then, but I'm in control of my faculties now." This appears to be true. Cocaine addiction feels like an intermittent insanity, followed by periods of partially sane behavior. The last portion of Step Two states we will be restored to sanity, not to a life that is half sane, half insane.

When addicts remain in recovery for an extended period of time, most come to believe that the power greater than themselves is a spiritual power, a power that initially helps them remain sober, but soon guides them in many aspects of life. Recovery is a continuing quest, a search for meaning. This search often leads to a new found spiritual significance in life. However, beginners need not focus on this goal today. When they take Step Two, they only need believe that a power greater than themselves will deliver them from drug addiction.

Step Three

Principle 5 — Step Three pushes the addict to shift the focus of control to a higher power.

Step Three states: *We made a decision to turn our will and our lives over to the care of God as we understood him.* An addict may believe he is powerless over his drug use, and that drugs have been a destructive force in his life. He may think that he does not have his own best interests at heart. He may believe that a power greater than himself is necessary to fix this problem. Nevertheless, most addicts are skeptical when they first encounter the idea of turning their lives over to someone or something else. The level of trust necessary *to turn our will and our lives over* makes Step Three a very difficult step for most. Initially, all that is required is willingness.

Trust often develops in stages. When an addict begins to trust his physician, counselor, or treatment team, he should let go of a small problem, and allow his treatment team to settle the outcome. Then, he should try turning over another small problem to his higher power and, over time, watch what happens. Through a series of successive attempts at trusting people and one's higher power, the addict prepares himself to turn his will and life over to his chosen higher power.

When the addict has deliberated long enough, Step Three encourages him to make a decision to turn his will and his life over to the care of God—as he understands him. Such a decision is not the result of a sudden insight or inspiration. If made with care, the decision of Step Three represents a turning point in recovery.

After taking Step Three, all addicts revert to taking control of their lives from time to time. This does not mean that they have failed to work Step Three. Step Three says we made a decision. It does not say we never took control again. The addict can return to piloting the ship at any time. However, if he has truly executed the third step, the addict will catch himself and quickly relinquish control because he has learned that his life does not work if he attempts to become his own "higher power."

Although the alcoholic may balk when asked to turn his will over to a higher power, the typical cocaine addict will make an impulsive toxic decision to take Step Three. While the alcoholic deliberates and often rebels against this step, the cocaine addict often makes a superficial assessment of Step Three and, unaware of the magnitude of the decision involved, acts impulsively. I encourage cocaine addicts to delay their decision to take Step Three, so that they may achieve the depth of understanding necessary to make a lasting commitment.

After the First Three Steps

By taking the first three steps, the addict will have experienced the heart of twelve-step recovery. Having done this, the addict must stop and review his mental and emotional state. If he has successfully begun the Twelve Steps, his position in life will have changed. Where there once was despair, there will be hope. Where there once was cynicism, there will be wonder. Where there once was shame, there will be a sensation of healing. If the addict does not experience these changes, he should return to Step One, and review his step work with his sponsor or counselor. Remember, there is no prize for being the fastest. The pay off in the Twelve Steps comes from careful consideration and commitment to each individual step. As the addict attends support groups, he may hear other addicts and alcoholics saying that they take the first three steps every day. This simply means they are reviewing their commitment to this vital element in recovery. People in early recovery should review their own commitments to each step at the start of every day. *The Cocaine Recovery Workbook* contains a daily review of the first three steps.

When a person feels that he has made progress on the first three steps, he should stop and begin planning for a life free from cocaine and other mood altering drugs. He need not rush ahead and try to complete the nine remaining steps. Most recovering addicts take one to three years to work the steps of recovery. Step work takes time!

The Cocaine Addiction Cycle describes a vicious cycle of cocaine use, alternating with periods of time away from the drug where the addict feels cured. During Stage IV, the drug problem may seem under control. The transformation that occurs through working the Twelve Steps will pull a person completely out of the addiction cycle. Through the experience of working the Twelve Steps, whether in a treatment center or out, the addict is removed from the recurring nightmare of cocaine addiction. The transformation, the shift out of addiction, occurs through the use and practice of the Twelve Steps.

Chapters One through Seven described the problems and pitfalls along the path of recovery. This chapter has introduced you to the path itself. I encourage all cocaine addicts and their families to use additional educational materials about the Twelve Steps. This book should supplement your reading in the A.A. book, *Twelve Steps and Twelve Traditions,* and other step literature.

Welcome to recovery!

NINE

Relapse Prevention

Principles

1. Relapse is a symptom of addiction; it is a characteristic of human beings, not a property of a drug.

2. Relapse can be viewed either as a singular event, or as a series of thoughts and behaviors that culminate in cocaine use.

3. Relapse into drug use does not indicate one has failed in recovery.

4. The simplest relapse-prevention techniques focus on eliminating certain relapse behaviors.

5. Understanding cocaine addiction decreases the probability of relapse. How the addict thinks about himself can decrease the possibility of relapse.

6. Almost every addict must change his lifestyle to recover.

7. When relapse is understood as a process, the addict can learn to recognize the warning signs that point to potential drug use.

Cocaine dependence, more than any other addictive disease, is charted by relapse. Relapse prevention should be a prime concern for all recovering cocaine addicts. The term relapse prevention encompasses all that can be done to prevent a return to drug and alcohol use. Relapse prevention includes: treatment, psychotherapy, education about addiction, twelve-step meeting attendance, relapse contracts, and drug screening.

It should also include subtle changes such as planning the use of leisure time, defining a new self-image as a recovering addict, and learning to handle emotions. This chapter describes additional techniques that prevent relapse as well. I encourage patients to work through each section in this chapter, and then complete the corresponding exercises in *The Cocaine Recovery Workbook.*

Relapse is defined as *the recurrence of symptoms of an illness after a period of improvement.* Addiction has many symptoms other than the consumption of drugs; any and all of these symptoms may indicate relapse. In the above definition of relapse is the clause: *after a period of improvement.* Relapse into a disease can only occur after a period of remission. If an addict leaves treatment, and on the way out the door uses alcohol or cocaine, this does not constitute a relapse. Rather, this is a treatment failure.

Relapse prevention is not a substitute for motivation in recovery. Relapse prevention is a group of techniques that help the motivated recovering addict remain drug-free.

Principle 1 — Relapse is a symptom of addiction; it is a characteristic of human beings, not a property of a drug.

The most startling finding about relapse is that the process of relapse is identical whether the drug is cocaine, alcohol, narcotics, or nicotine. The timing, behaviors, thoughts, and rationalizations that lead to relapse are the same whether the addiction arises from chemical use, an eating disorder, compulsive gambling, or compulsive sexuality. Relapse is a process that occurs in human beings when they fall into addictive behaviors, not a property contained in a white powder or a bottle of alcohol. Each type of addictive illness has a distinct set of cues that can trigger a relapse. However, once these cues are activated, the behaviors and thoughts that culminate in a recurrence of the addiction are the same, irrespective of the type of addictive disease.

Principle 2 — Relapse can be viewed either as a singular event, or as a series of thoughts and behaviors that culminate in cocaine use.

There are two distinct ways to view a relapse. The simplest way of viewing relapse is as a singular event untied to past or future. I once treated an alcoholic who returned to treatment after many years of sobriety. He was quite intoxicated and bewildered to be back in treatment. I asked him how he wound up drinking again, and he replied, "Well, Doc, I just found myself in a bar with a drink in my hand!" This is an extreme example of the view that relapse is an event, a singular point in time, with no precedents.

A second, more dynamic way of viewing a relapse is as a series of thoughts, behaviors, and feelings that slowly escalate, eventually culminating in drug use. This method of viewing relapse is called the process model. This model is more complex, and as a result, process-based relapse-prevention techniques are complex as well. By viewing relapse as a process—one that takes from ten minutes to ten months to evolve—an addict gives himself time to intervene prior to returning to drug use.

It is helpful to view relapse with both the event and process perspectives. I will first discuss the event perspective, defining specific behaviors, ways of thinking, lifestyle changes, and craving management techniques. When the addict has a firm hold on the events that produce relapse, he should be well on his way to a relapse-prevention program. Then I will describe the process model of relapse. The process of relapse may be composed of any number of relapse events, giving the addict any number of opportunities for intervention prior to cocaine use.

The process model describes a road an addict may travel *even after he has begun his journey in recovery*. Like the path of recovery, certain events place the addict on the road to relapse and others speed him along the way. All cocaine addicts will flip from the recovery path to the relapse road from time to time during recovery. It is imperative for the addict to learn how to recognize the characteristics of a pending relapse and thus prevent the final event—a cocaine binge.

Principle 3 — Relapse into drug use does not indicate one has failed in recovery.

What happens to an addict who leaves treatment, and begins on the road to relapse? He recognizes that he has switched from the recovery path to the relapse road. He is worried that he may use cocaine. He struggles with cocaine cravings and finally gives in.

At this point the addict must recognize his relapse. What he does with this fact is much more important than the fact that he did relapse. Statistics show that the majority of cocaine addicts return to cocaine use at least once. This statistic does not have to apply to everyone. On the other hand, the statistics indicate that it is imperative for every addict to have a set of procedures available that extract him from the downhill spiral of cocaine use, should it ever occur. If an addict relapses, he should get up, dust himself off, and walk away questioning why the relapse happened. He should return immediately to his treatment program and support groups, and talk to others about the relapse. If he feels shame, he must talk about this too. Shame will only prevent him from learning from the relapse event. The addict learns more about recovery by processing a relapse than he learns through any other treatment experience—if he returns to his program.

Event-Based Relapse Prevention

Our study of relapse prevention begins by examining events that precipitate relapse. Most of the event-based techniques have universal application. They fall into four categories that should be reviewed along with the corresponding sections in *The Cocaine Recovery Workbook*. The four categories of event-based techniques are:

   1. Behavioral techniques

   2. Cognitive techniques

   3. Lifestyle modification techniques

   4. Craving management techniques

Behavioral techniques

Principle 4 — The simplest relapse-prevention techniques focus on eliminating certain relapse behaviors.

Behavioral techniques relate to specific behaviors that reduce the probability of relapse. Behavioral techniques are simple and, when followed precisely, they provide direct and effective methods of avoiding relapse.

Some behavioral techniques decrease the possibility of being exposed to cocaine. When the addict physically removes himself from the presence of cocaine, the probability of relapse decreases dramatically. Examples of reducing cocaine access include:

- Remove all cocaine and all cocaine paraphernalia from one's house.
- Stop any cocaine and other drug dealing.
- Throw away all phone numbers of cocaine dealers.
- Write letters to all cocaine-using friends indicating that if they come around with cocaine, the police will be called.
- Insure that one's paycheck gets to the bank via direct deposit.
- Avoid carrying around large sums of money.
- Throw away the automatic teller bank card.
- Do not drive in the neighborhood where one's drug dealer lives.
- Change residence and job location if one is exposed to drug use in either location.
- Do not return to a spouse who is addicted.

A cocaine addict with a willingness to do all these things is indeed sincere about recovery. Most of the above list is self-explanatory. Several of the behaviors involve removing cocaine or cocaine reminders from sight. Addicts must destroy all drug paraphernalia. The only reason to keep paraphernalia is to use drugs. Some people have specific places in their city or town where they used drugs exclusively. These locations should be avoided for the first six months of recovery. If one must return for any reason, he should go with recovering friends at his side.

Other behaviors involve access to money. Because cocaine is expensive, addicts associate having money with having cocaine. Money (especially cash) can trigger a cocaine craving. A decrease in the availability of cash will decrease the probability of cocaine purchase and cash-induced craving. Direct deposit of paychecks may prevent the "payday binge" that typifies many cocaine users.

Most cocaine addicts use alone or with close associates. If an addict has made a commitment to stop using cocaine, this commitment should be important to his good friends as well. Genuine friends, who may still use cocaine occasionally, will not tempt the recovering addict by coming around him when they are using. There are other so-called friends who see the recovering addict and say, "Well, a little bit won't hurt" or "You were not serious about completely stopping were you?" These so-called friends hope the addict will return to drug use. These people are probably addicted to cocaine as well and either they need someone to use with, or they need someone to buy cocaine for them. These people will drift away when they realize they are getting nowhere.

Working in a job where there is ready access to cocaine presents a serious problem. Many addicts may find it necessary to change jobs. Changing jobs may mean moving to a different location in the company, working different hours, or simply quitting. This may seem like an extreme measure, but I firmly believe that many addicts find jobs, and friends at these jobs, just to increase their access to cocaine. When the addict begins recovery, he needs to examine his motives for working where he works.

Many cocaine addicts have spouses or close relationships with others who use cocaine and other drugs. It is very difficult for one half of a couple to stop using cocaine while the other half continues to use. An addict who returns to a spouse who uses cocaine is setting himself up for relapse. A recovering addict should either get his or her spouse into treatment or move out until it is safe for the addict to return. Commonly, when a person develops his own sobriety away from a using spouse, he will return home to find that the only thing they had in common was drug use and addiction.

In addition to avoiding negative situations, behavioral relapse-prevention techniques utilize positive behaviors as well. Positive behaviors occur when addicts:

- Attend twelve-step meetings on a regular basis.
- Spend time with friends who do not use drugs, or with friends in recovery.
- Obtain proper sleep, eat balanced meals, and exercise regularly (things one neglects when using).
- Develop leisure activities that are not associated with drug use.
- Find self-esteem in areas other than drugs and the cocaine culture.

Where does one go to avoid cocaine? The answer is simple: twelve-step meetings. And when not in meetings, the addict should spend time with friends in recovery, or with friends who do not have an addiction problem.

Other positive behaviors concern developing and maintaining physical health. When engaged in the Cocaine Addiction Cycle, the user alternates periods of no sleep and poor food intake with periods of moderate to heavy food intake and long reflexive sleeps. While using, the addict consumes poor quality food. Vitamin and nutritional deficiencies are common (see Chapter Four). The sleep cycle is deeply disturbed by erratic sleep patterns. The only exercise most cocaine addicts get is running for more drugs, or running around in circles in anxious desperation during a binge. Poor sleep, poor nutritional habits, and no helpful exercise are part of being a cocaine addict. Recovery is assisted by correcting these problems with regular sleep, sound nutrition, and participation in regular exercise.

Sleeping is more than just a rest. Alternating waking with sleeping in a regular pattern entrains one's circadian rhythms.

A regular circadian rhythm decreases the tendency toward depression. Each person has their own variation of sleep and waking needs. Most people need between five and eight and one half hours of sleep a night. When an addict determines his sleep needs, he should sleep a consistent time from night to night. He should eat regular nutritious meals throughout the day. An addict's energy will return as he replaces the nutrients depleted by drug and alcohol use. If a recovering addict needs help devising a balanced diet, he should talk to a dietician, nurse, or physician about a diet that is low in simple sugars and fat, high in complex carbohydrates, protein, and fiber. An eating disorder such as anorexia nervosa, bulimia nervosa, or compulsive overeating should be addressed early in treatment (see Chapter Ten).

Exercise is an important part of recovery. Chronic cocaine consumption makes the heart beat rapidly and decreases the efficiency of the heart's pumping action. This increases the possibility of heart failure and heart attacks later in life. Aerobic exercise increases the heart's efficiency. All cocaine addicts who are medically stable should participate in regular exercise. Regular exercise also combats the anhedonic depression that results from cocaine use. Exercise decreases restless feelings in early recovery. Exercise is also part of leisure and having fun.

At first, most recovering addicts have difficulties having fun in recovery. Leisure without drugs takes effort. Everyone in treatment for addiction should develop a leisure plan that includes some exciting activities and some sedate ones. Some people feel awkward returning to old leisure activities. When a recovering addict engages in leisure activities, he should talk to others about how he feels. Encouragement from others will follow. Low self-esteem is a fact in early recovery. I instruct cocaine addicted patients to develop a list of activities and behaviors that will help them improve the low self-esteem that accompanies early recovery.

The exercises in *The Cocaine Recovery Workbook* address each of the negative behaviors to avoid, and the positive behaviors to develop as part of a relapse-prevention plan. Such a plan will help an addict avoid cocaine as well as improve the quality of his life.

Cognitive techniques

Principle 5 — Understanding cocaine addiction decreases the probability of relapse. How the addict thinks about himself can decrease the possibility of relapse.

Cognitive relapse-prevention techniques are ways of thinking that prevent a return to drug use. Cognitive techniques do not rely on feelings. Rather, they are ways that addicts can perceive or understand themselves that help them recover. For an example of cognitive relapse prevention, read Chapter Two on the medical complications of cocaine use, and pay attention to how you feel about cocaine. As the addict learns about the complications of cocaine addiction, he will begin to think and feel differently about cocaine use. To a large degree, reading this book is employing a cognitive relapse-prevention technique. Though cognitive techniques alone will not make one recover, when the journey of recovery is begun, cognitive techniques make the recovery path smoother.

I will discuss three specific cognitive relapse-prevention techniques in this chapter:

1. Establishing in the mind that the first hit of cocaine or the first drink of alcohol rekindles addiction.

2. Learning about the consequences of drug use, and accepting that it can and did happen to you.

3. Redefining oneself as a nonuser.

4. Understanding, accepting, and not falling prey to euphoric recall (see Chapter Six for a complete discussion of euphoric recall and cognitive techniques for handling euphoric recall).

Most cocaine addicts who have never been exposed to treatment believe the major problem with cocaine is that they always use too much. Such an addict might say "I would have been O.K. if I had not used that second half gram." As addiction progresses, it becomes apparent that the trouble really begins with the first hit of cocaine. Most addicts, however, do not want to know this. When they arrive in treatment, most addicts say they want to learn to control—not stop—their use. One of the primary goals of treatment is to convince the addict that casual cocaine use is not possible. Animal research verifies that all animals, including human beings once they are addicted, can only use cocaine in a compulsive fashion.

Knowing and believing that casual cocaine use is not possible is a cognitive relapse-prevention technique. If an addict stops trying to finagle an occasional bump of cocaine, he will eventually stop toying with the idea of using at all. The cognitive shift occurs when the addict visualizes himself as someone who cannot use cocaine successfully. The goal of relapse prevention becomes avoiding the first hit.

Next, the addict must learn about the consequences of drug use, and accept that addiction can and did happen to him. All addicts should review the physical, emotional, and spiritual consequences of their addiction. Cocaine addiction, in particular, induces a subtle and pervasive form of denial (see Chapter Six). The addict should catalog all of the consequences of his drug use, and return to review and update this catalog periodically throughout his treatment and recovery. When the addict knows in his heart that he has suffered at the hands of his cocaine addiction, he will be less likely to relapse.

A final cognitive technique worth discussion is the exercise defining oneself as a nonuser. People entering treatment and recovery tend to believe that they will no longer have fun because they have stopped using drugs and alcohol. A clear voice from within says, "The party is over!" Addicts associate alcohol and drug use with fun, even after being devastated by their addiction. Some of this association is induced by our society. In the media, fun and recreation are almost always associated with alcohol use. A deeper association comes from using mind-altering substances for so long that the brain correlates alcohol and drug use with enjoyment. As a result, early recovery often feels like a joyless period or an endurance test.

When an addict reenters social activities, he will carry with him the belief that he is unable to have fun. This belief blocks the addict from permitting himself to enjoy his sober leisure activities. To correct this, the addict must expose himself to recreational activities so that, with time, he will be able to relax and enjoy them. By forcing himself to have sober fun, he will begin to appreciate the pleasure of recreation in recovery.

Watching someone drink a beer may create envy. Even an old cocaine-using friend, half-whacked from cocaine, can produce jealousy. Envy and jealousy make the addict feel deprived. Experiencing these feelings of deprivation over a long time is nerve wracking and can drive an addict to relapse. The simplest way to decrease the feeling of deprivation is to conceptualize oneself as a nonuser. People who do not use drugs do not spend time longing for them. The cognitive relapse-prevention technique consists of the addict thinking of himself as someone who does not use drugs anymore, rather than as someone who is trying hard to avoid the inevitable relapse. For those who work hard at recovery, the initial feelings of deprivation will disappear, usually within the first year.

Lifestyle changes

Principle 6 — Almost every addict must change his lifestyle to recover.

Using drugs, especially cocaine, changes the addict's lifestyle. If he was once careful with money, he now becomes careless. If he was honest, he begins to lie. If once he went to bed early, now he stays out all night looking for more cocaine. Once he had caring friends, but now all he has are acquaintances who only care about cocaine. Most lifestyle changes evolve to perpetuate the use of cocaine. The addict's subconscious mind creates the drug-based lifestyle. The subconscious mind changes viewpoints and attitudes to insure that the addict has ready access to drugs. The longer the addict is involved in drug and alcohol use, the more the subconscious mind has changed perspectives and attitudes to foster the drug lifestyle.

Individuals who have gone down hill rapidly have fewer permutations in lifestyle than those who have been using drugs and alcohol for many years. In the latter case, values and relationships have often been completely altered by addiction. In the extreme, addicts who have used drugs continuously since their early teens do not know anything about a drug-free lifestyle and social set. These people need to learn for the first time how to interact with others in a meaningful way. The extent of lifestyle degradation determines the amount of rehabilitation that is needed for a healthy recovery.

Early in treatment, the addict is apt to underestimate the effect of subtle changes in his lifestyle. He may even believe that his cocaine addiction is not reflected in his lifestyle at all. This is always incorrect. Pharmacists occasionally decide to go to pharmacy school to be near drugs. Physicians have been known to chose a specific medical specialty to be close to certain drugs. Many addicts who work in bars or deal cocaine make excuses such as "I won't turn out like my customers," not realizing that they have already arrived at that point. Addicted individuals make decisions about career, education, and marriage that are all driven by their addicted subconscious mind.

Recovery repairs the lifestyle changes that develop during cocaine use. In early recovery, a person will need to examine many facets of his lifestyle. If he continues in a drug-use lifestyle, he will relapse despite his best intentions to remain sober. An addict should examine all areas of his life with his sponsor, physician, or treatment providers, and search out behaviors and attitudes that promote relapse. Some lifestyles promote cocaine use and deserve special attention:

- Any addict who sells drugs needs to stop such activity at once. Even if the cocaine addict does not return to cocaine himself, which is unlikely, dealing cocaine can not in any way be construed to be a lifestyle consistent with recovery.

- Cocaine addicts who are successful in recovery rarely work in nightclubs or bars. Such jobs almost always involve drug exchange and drug use. At the very least, the atmosphere in such places promotes alcohol dependency. Recovering cocaine addicts who did not drink prior to treatment quickly develop alcoholism if they drink alcohol while trying to recover. Alcohol consumption in a cocaine addict often leads to cocaine use. Therefore, recovering addicts should move out of such jobs as soon as possible.

- Individuals in extremely stressful jobs such as high-pressure sales, real estate, the stock market and advertising are often unable to maintain sobriety. In fact, cocaine addicts often select work that is glamorous and involves large sums of money; it seems to be in synchrony with the high-pressure they experience while using. Recovering addicts should attempt to shift to a less stressful job in the same line of work or change professions.

- A recovering cocaine addict has no business living with an active alcoholic or drug-addicted individual. A recovering person who is in a close relationship with an addict should strongly consider remaining in residential care away from that significant other for a period of time. During this time, reasonable demands can be proffered, each aimed at leading the significant other into his or her own recovery. If these attempts are not successful, the recovering addict should consider breaking off the relationship. Although this may seem drastic, it will prevent an almost certain return to drug use.

- While they were using, some addicts chose a job working with other addicts. They entered a plant or job and thought, "Gee, these are my type of people," unaware that *my type* means cocaine addicts and dealers. When in recovery, these addicts need to consider finding a new job or job location.

- The addict should also examine his choice of companions. Does he play sports, engage in hobbies, or socialize with people who drink heavily or use drugs? The addict must question if he has self-selected his friends to be cocaine and alcohol users. If so, he must eliminate these friends and share these activities with recovering friends.

- If an addict's career path was determined during a prolonged period of drug or alcohol usage, the career path should be very closely investigated. It is possible that a specific career was chosen subconsciously in order to insure the addict had ready access to drugs and alcohol. Or he may have chosen an undemanding or unsupervised job that would not interfere with his drug or alcohol consumption.

In early recovery, any new job or social situation should be carefully assessed as well. Is the new job stressful or does it involve excess exposure to alcohol or drugs? Is the situation similar to the one the addict just left in order to avoid relapse? If so, the addict is best served by continuing the search for work that promotes his recovery.

Often, lifestyle changes begin when an addict meets a new set of friends at twelve-step recovery groups. These friends introduce beginners to new ways of relating to each other in recovery. Many treatment programs have active alumni associations and continuing care groups that provide access to individuals who are experiencing the same issues in life and provide a set of friends for the addict new to recovery.

The Process Model of Relapse

Principle 7 — When relapse is understood as a process, the addict can learn to recognize the warning signs that point to potential drug use.

Relapse rarely falls out of the sky without warning. Relapse begins as a series of minor thoughts, feelings and behaviors that escalate over time. For the chemically dependent person, relapse is a process that culminates in drug or alcohol use. Just as there is a path to recovery, there is a road to relapse. In this section we will develop an understanding of that road.

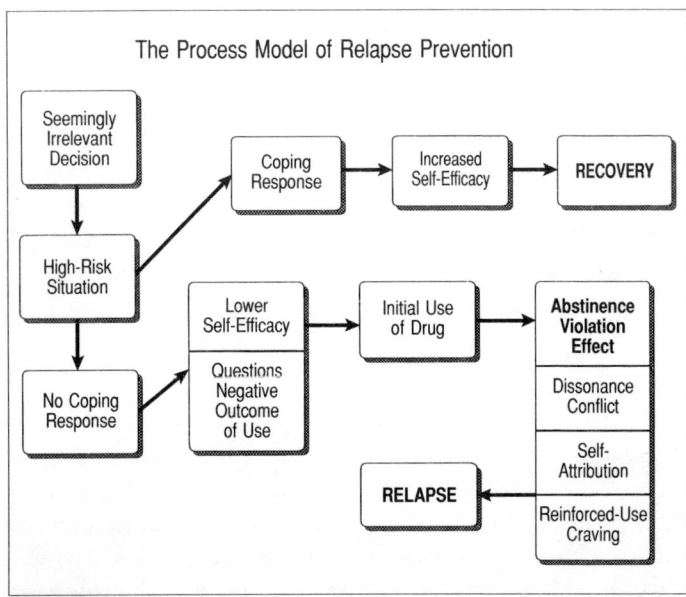

Figure 9
The process model of relapse prevention describes relapse as a series of events, decisions, and emotions. Many events occur before the addict uses drugs or alcohol. When an addict views relapse as a process, he has many opportunities to stop relapse before it culminates in drug use.

Recovering addicts ask me "Will I ever relapse?" To which I reply, "Everyone in recovery will, from time to time, find themselves on the road to relapse." Some cocaine addicts will return to drug and alcohol use, and thus complete the relapse process. When an addict prevents cocaine use, he moves off the relapse road.

The process model of relapse was first described by Judith Gordon and Alan Marlatt in 1976. I have adopted and modified their model for cocaine addiction. This relapse model describes all the characteristics of relapse from the first thoughts to the final cocaine binge. Figure 9 explains the process model as modified from Marlatt and Gordon's original work.

When one looks at a relapse—"I found myself in a bar with a drink in my hand"—it is not important what was ordered, or how much was consumed, or if cash was used to pay for the drink. What *is* important is how the addict got in the bar in the first place. The relapse occurred when he gave himself permission to perform all the behaviors that culminated in the drink meeting his lips. Intervention in this series of complex behaviors comprises the process of relapse prevention. If the addict understands the behaviors that lead to the actual cocaine or alcohol use, he decreases the probability of drug relapse.

Each of the stages of the relapse road will be described, followed by an example of the relapse process.

The components of relapse

A relapse begins with a *Seemingly Irrelevant Decision* (SID). Seemingly irrelevant decisions are small choices that appear on the surface to have no impact whatever on an addiction problem. When an addict makes a SID, his subconscious mind has pushed him to make a small decision that increases his vulnerability to relapse. For example, a recovering addict may decide to drive home from work a different way. The choice of a new route home is a SID. On the way home, it seems coincidental that he is driving through the neighborhood where he used to buy cocaine. The addict's SID has placed him on the relapse road. Everyone makes thousands of decisions each day. Some of them are SIDs that make relapse possible.

Seemingly irrelevant decisions place one in *high-risk situations*. High-risk situations are physical, emotional, or spiritual situations where an addict is likely to use. For example, a high-risk situation occurs when an addict drives through the neighborhood where he used cocaine. He begins to think about his drug dealer as he drives down familiar streets. He has vague thoughts about using and begins to detect his cold sweaty palms and racing heart. The addict then recognizes the danger of relapse. His SID (to take a different route home) has placed him in a high-risk situation (driving past his dealer's house). In shifting from a SID to a high-risk situation, the relapse process moves from the subconscious mind to the conscious mind.

A high-risk situation is a major turning point on the road to relapse. The addict can take corrective action—in this case—

leaving the neighborhood. This is called a *coping response*, as shown in Figure 9. If an addict makes a coping response, he feels increasingly effective in his recovery, which decreases the possibility of relapse down the road. By moving out of a high-risk situation with a coping response, the addict learns that relapse is not inevitable.

If, on the other hand, the addict remains in a high-risk situation for too long, his addiction develops a stronger voice in his head. He begins rationalizing his dilemma, "Just one hit won't hurt." And then, "I feel better about myself so I won't let myself get out of control." He also begins to romanticize the outcome of using: "I haven't used in so long; it will feel good!" The combination of romanticizing and rationalizing makes the addict believe that using cocaine will result in a positive outcome. The addict also feels he has lost control of his behavior, as if his thoughts and feelings conspired to place him in his current situation. Expecting a positive outcome and feeling less effective at controlling his behavior places the addict at the next stage in the relapse process.

If nothing positive is done at this stage, the addict will use cocaine. Once the addict has had the first hit, it is almost impossible for him stop using. The drive to use more is overwhelming. The use of a small quantity of any drug produces the *Abstinence Violation Effect* (AVE). This effect is a combination of the neurobiology of cocaine and the psychology of addiction. The three components of the AVE are dissonance conflict, self-attribution, and the neurochemical effect of cocaine on the brain. All three components of the AVE collude to escalate the initial use of cocaine into a prolonged binge.

The first component of the AVE is *dissonance conflict*. Dissonance conflict is a thinking problem, a cognitive process. The addict felt he was doing well in his recovery. Yet, here he sits with cocaine in his hands. The conflict between his perception of how he was doing ("I am a recovering addict") and his current reality creates an anxious confusion ("What is this cocaine doing in front of me?"). The conflict drives him to continue his drug use.

The second component of the AVE is *self-attribution*. If the addict is truly invested in recovery and uses cocaine just once, he will begin to say angry things to himself, such as "All this time I was fooling myself; I really wanted to use." The self-blame brings a hopeless air to the using situation, driving the addict further into relapse.

The third component of the AVE is *reinforced-use craving*. This is the biological process whereby cocaine reinforces its own continued consumption (as described in Chapter Five). When the addict uses cocaine, his biologic drive is to use more. His craving escalates drug use, which in turn creates more reinforced-use craving. This vicious cycle pushes the addict further into relapse.

These three components of the AVE combine to complete a relapse. When the first binge occurs, the addict will most likely fall back into the Cocaine Addiction Cycle. However, it is possible to exit from the road to relapse at many points along the way. I will discuss these points later. For now, let us discuss an example of a relapse process.

A relapse example

Michael is a recovering cocaine and alcohol addict who has completed an extended-care treatment program. He has been living in a recovery residence for over three months and feels very solid about his recovery program. Michael has found other things to do with his time besides using alcohol and drugs.

One day, Michael decides to attend a baseball game with some old friends. He knows these friends do not have alcohol or drug problems. They do, however, occasionally drink beer. These friends pick Michael up at his apartment on a hot summer day. In the car on the way to the game Michael considers whether or not to tell his friends about his cocaine dependence. While riding in the car he makes a seemingly irrelevant decision (SID), "I don't have to tell them about this drug thing; they never knew me when I was using drugs.

Besides, they're not addicts and won't be a bad influence." In his shame, Michael hides this information from his friends. Michael was worried about his friends' response to his addiction and recovery.

This seemingly irrelevant decision has far reaching consequences. The three friends go to the baseball stadium and decide to sit in the bleachers. The game begins, and one of Michael's friends decides to have a beer. Suddenly, Michael's healthy recreation has shifted to a high-risk situation. Early in recovery, Michael is exposed to beer on a hot day.

Now that Michael is in a high-risk situation, he has two options. One is to develop a coping response to sitting next to someone drinking beer. He may say, "Gee, let me tell you about what I have been doing lately. I just completed a treatment program for alcohol and cocaine dependence. My treatment providers tell me that it is a good idea not to be around anyone who is drinking alcohol when I am early in recovery." Michael's friend (who does not have an alcohol problem) gets up and throws out the beer saying "I'm glad you let me know; I wouldn't want to threaten your recovery!" Michael breathes a sigh of relief, and offers to buy his friend a soft drink.

If Michael responds in this manner to the high-risk situation, he has made a coping response. This increases his self-efficacy, and decreases the probability that Michael will relapse in the future. When an addict sets limits, minor as they may seem, he will feel increasingly effective at setting limits later. The next exposure to alcohol, drugs, or relapse situations may be more dangerous.

Michael's second option in this high-risk situation is to do nothing. He may decide not to tell his friends about his treatment and recovery. Instead, he sits uneasily in his bleacher chair. Michael soon finds himself fantasizing about how good a beer would taste on this hot summer day. He chastises himself for not speaking out, "Why can't I tell them about my past?" He berates himself for the fix he is in. Meanwhile, the smell of

Relapse Prevention

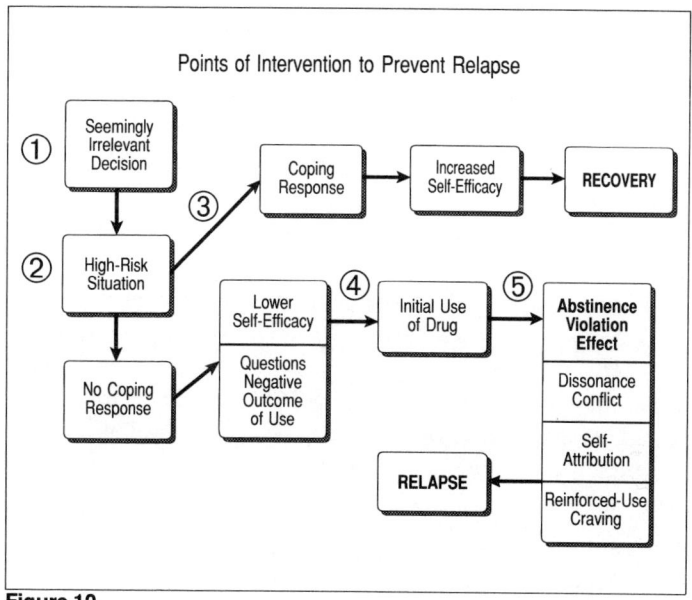

Figure 10
Using the process model of relapse prevention, we can define places along the road to relapse where one can abort the relapse process, and thus prevent drug use.

beer exacerbates Michael's craving until he impulsively asks his friend for a sip of beer. Michael moves to the next stage of the relapse process—he has used an initial amount of alcohol. Initial substance use creates the abstinence violation effect.

The abstinence violation effect produces a cascade of sensations. Michael calls himself stupid, and feels that he is a fool for not taking better care of himself. Michael blames himself for his failure so soon after leaving the recovery residence (self-attribution). His first sip of beer has led him to buy his own beer. His friends do not say anything, as they do not know he is in recovery. Michael sits in the bleacher chair with a beer in his hand, staring down at the glass. His harsh internal self, a voice inside his head yells: "What are you doing?" The difference in how he felt he was doing in recovery ("I thought I had such a good program") and his current situation is very discomforting ("If I'm doing so well, what am I doing with a beer in my hand?"). This is cognitive dissonance; it produces tension and discomfort. The tension and discomfort, in turn, accelerate the relapse. These two components of the abstinence violation effect are added to a third. The alcohol quiets the harsh voice in his head, the voice that screams about relapse. Michael continues to drink, attempting to calm the war raging inside of him. The effect of alcohol on the mind is the third, and most powerful, regulator of continued use in a relapse.

When Michael has consumed three beers, he feels overwhelmed, excited, and shameful. The alcohol in his system ignites cocaine craving and he becomes obsessed with thoughts of using cocaine. Michael buys cocaine. This leads to a full blown relapse. Once he uses cocaine, he will most likely reenter the Cocaine Addiction Cycle to complete the relapse process.

Points of intervention in the process model

What does one do to avoid relapse? There are several points of intervention on the relapse road. They appear in Figure 10 as:

1. Preventing oneself from acting on a seemingly irrelevant decision.

2. Avoiding high-risk situations.

3. Developing coping mechanisms for high-risk situations.

4. Preventing the initial use of drugs or alcohol.

5. Stopping the Abstinence Violation Effect from occurring once the addict has used an initial amount of cocaine or another drug.

The further along in the relapse process, the more difficult it is to avoid drug use. Therefore, it is preferable for the addict to catch himself before he reaches the fourth point of intervention in the model shown in Figure 10. Let us discuss each of the points of intervention in order.

The first prevention point is recognizing and avoiding seemingly irrelevant decisions. Though not all relapses start with a SID, I teach patients to be suspicious of their motives. Beginners in sobriety should examine their plans on a hourly basis, because they are either working toward or away from the next hit of cocaine. Decisions not to sell a car, not to throw away using music, or to continue a casual sexual relationship with a using partner are good examples of seemingly irrelevant decisions. Because seemingly irrelevant decisions are hard to detect, I recommend that addicts in early recovery live with recovering friends. These friends often see the danger in certain decisions when the addict himself cannot. A rehabilitation counselor or a twelve-step sponsor can also confront the addict about a SID before it leads to a high-risk situation.

The second point of intervention in the relapse process is avoiding high-risk situations. *The Cocaine Recovery Workbook* has exercises to help the addict identify high-risk situations. High-risk situations can be places, individuals, or activities that may lead to drug use. High-risk situations may be emotions: anger, sadness, and excitement early in recovery can trigger drug use. When developing a list of high-risk situations, the addict should keep the list with him through the day. When he discovers or remembers additional situations, they should be added to the list. Then the addict needs to discuss and develop a specific plan for each one of his high-risk situations. The list may be quite long, but should be complete; this is a critical exercise in relapse prevention.

The third technique is implemented after the addict finds himself in a high-risk situation. An effective coping response must be enacted at once to avoid drug use. Long before a person begins to consider using alcohol or drugs, he must take an aggressive stance. As stated earlier, a coping response demands that an addict set limits for himself and for those around him. A coping response may involve physically removing oneself from a location where alcohol and drugs are being consumed. The addict may need to tell others that he will not tolerate drug use around him. A coping response may also involve consciously attempting to change a vulnerable emotional state.

The fourth area of intervention in the process of relapse occurs when the addict stops a relapse just prior to drug use. This is an alarm point. If the addict is in a high-risk situation and fails to develop a coping response, he will probably use. The most effective technique at this point is to run as one would from a forest fire.

The fifth and final point of prevention is stopping the relapse after the initial use of a substance. Stopping a cocaine binge after it has started is very difficult. However, the addict can call a sponsor, throw the cocaine down the sink, and leave the scene of drug use. This will cut the cocaine binge short. If the relapse started with alcohol, rather than cocaine, it may be easier to stop. It is crucial to develop a "no surrender" attitude toward addiction. Being angry at oneself for initial use does nothing to stop subsequent drug use. One drink of alcohol or one hit of cocaine does not indicate failure in recovery. It *is* a setback in the twelve-step recovery program—what matters is what one *does* with the relapse, not that the relapse occurred.

Drug Screening in Recovery

Drug screening can be a help in recovery. Results of random witnessed drug screens can be reported to the addict, his spouse, his employer, or to a licensing authority. Random drug screens need specific components to be effective. These components are:

- Testing must be truly random. The screen should occur on a random date within each time period.
- After being notified, the addict must appear for testing within 24 hours. If he does not show up for a drug test, it is counted as a positive result.
- All screens should be witnessed. If unwitnessed, samples need to be tested for specific gravity and urine temperature.
- The specimen bottle must be sealed in front of the patient, and transported by a known chain of custody. This simply means that each person who carries the urine sample attests to proper specimen handling.

- All specimens must be tested by one method and confirmed by a second, preferably an emission type of radioimmunoassay (EMIT-RIA) or gas chromatography/mass spectroscopy (GC/MS). This book is not the place to describe these techniques. An addict should simply know these terms so he is able to ask for them in his urine testing.

This information about proper drug screening techniques is for everyone's protection. With proper screening all concerned individuals can be assured of drug abstinence.

Most patients balk at the prospect of random screening when I introduce the concept to them. However, random screening is useful. In treatment, random screening confirms that every patient in the treatment program is drug-free. In the maintenance phase of treatment and in continuing care, random drug screens are one more roadblock in preventing relapse. Many patients return for a follow-up appointment and say: "I had a bad craving episode, and thought about using, but I knew you might catch me with a drug test. I just held on, and soon the craving just left!" Because drug screens verify that a person is drug-free, suspicions about possible drug use are often laid to rest. If an accident occurs at the job, or if there is an argument at home, random tests will confirm that the addict has remained drug-free. Drug screening provides a sense of security, and in many cases they are required. Those who do not intend to use cocaine have nothing to fear.

A positive drug screen should push the addict back into a refresher course of treatment. One positive test should not be a reason to be fired from a job or to lose a license. A program of random drug screening is of best use if maintained over the first two to three years of recovery.

TEN

Long-Term Therapy and Cocaine

Principles

1. Not everyone in recovery needs psychotherapy.

2. Recovering addicts should search carefully for the right therapist.

3. Many cocaine addicts have problems with eating disorders, intimacy, or sexual addiction.

4. Cocaine addicts in recovery suffer from destructive emotional cycles similar to the Cocaine Addiction Cycle.

5. Many cocaine addicts have problems with too much or too little ego.

6. The success/failure complex is created when cocaine addiction is combined with certain preexisting psychological problems.

7. Some addicts in recovery need additional therapy to cope with feelings of restlessness or emptiness.

Some people have emotional problems long before they are exposed to cocaine. Others develop distorted feelings about themselves, their sexuality, their goals in life, or their relationships due to addiction. Every addict has some emotional problems as a result of using cocaine. Early in recovery, most addicts try to blame their drug problems on their emotional problems. This chapter is not for anyone who is still maintaining that their emotional distress, at times, warrants using cocaine. Denial of this kind is discussed in Chapter Six.

Principle 1 — Not everyone in recovery needs psychotherapy.

After cocaine use has stopped and the addict has entered a twelve-step program, he is still apt to carry some emotional baggage from his past. The first avenue of treatment is always through the Twelve Steps. This baggage is addressed head on by Steps Four through Nine. Problems of childhood, adolescence, and the years spent using drugs may be unearthed by Steps Four and Five. The addict then learns to tolerate or release these problems in Steps Six and Seven. Interpersonal problems are addressed in Steps Eight and Nine. The remainder of the Twelve Steps provides recovery maintenance and spiritual growth.

After a time in recovery, many addicts find they continue to have difficulty adjusting to life. People who have been emotionally, physically, or sexually abused need additional help. People who want to believe their childhoods were idyllic, but suffer emotional scars from their early life need therapy to bring these problems to light. People who are going to twelve-step meetings, are talking with their sponsors, and are attending the continuing care phase of treatment may still feel empty inside, hopeless about the future, or afraid to change. These people need additional psychotherapy. People enter treatment to get straight and sober and to feel better about themselves. An addict should find contentment in recovery. If an addict is involved in recovery and still feels that his life is sad or bleak, psychotherapy is recommended.

Many problems in recovery stem from the use of cocaine. Many other problems in recovering addicts were present long before they began using cocaine. People are often tempted to differentiate between problems that arose prior to cocaine use and those that were created by addiction. Although this exercise is interesting, it is of little clinical value. It is usually a waste of valuable therapy time.

Intensive psychotherapy with a cocaine addict outside of a treatment setting should begin only after he has obtained six to eight months of solid abstinence from cocaine use. Psychotherapy is different from the supportive treatment provided by continuing care programs and support groups. It is disturbing, unnerving, and anxiety provoking. Much of the growth in psychotherapy comes from the discomfort it produces, therefore it should be delayed until the individual has settled into a recovery program.

Of the many forms of therapy, group therapy has proven to most often benefit recovering addicts. Group therapy provides varying points of view, corrects distortions about life, and gives a recovering addict an opportunity to work through his problems with other people in his past and present. An addict's feelings about his parents may arise when another group member begins to talk. An addict may learn to trust others when his group confronts him about dangerous behavior without shaming or invalidating him. In this manner, group therapy frequently gives the addict more than individual therapy can give.

In some cases individual therapy is recommended. Issues that are too disturbing to bring to a group are often best uncovered in individual therapy. However, such painful issues are best healed if they are subsequently brought up in a group setting.

Principle 2 — Recovering addicts should search carefully for the right therapist.

If an addict needs therapy, he should search for a therapist who understands addiction and is capable of treating recovering patients. If the potential therapist is a physician, the addict should look for a physician who has an active practice in psychotherapy, and who is very cautious about giving *any* medications to recovering addicts.

I recommend that a prospective patient talk to a therapist for several sessions before deciding to begin therapy in earnest. During initial talks, the patient should evaluate the therapist as much as the therapist evaluates the addict. I recommend two criteria to judge a potential therapist.

- First, the potential therapist must understand the trauma of addiction and understand how a twelve-step program promotes healing. When the addict talks with a prospective therapist and describes his past experiences with cocaine, the addict should pay attention to his inner feelings. Do these feelings confirm that this potential therapist understands the trauma of addiction? At this stage in recovery the addict should be able to trust his instincts to tell him if this therapist will be helpful in his recovery. Therapists who are also in recovery from alcohol or drug addictions may be a good choice for psychotherapy. The addict should not, however, use this as the sole criterion for choosing his therapist.

- Second, the therapist must have experience or training in areas where the patient has problems. If shame was an issue as a child, the therapist must know about emotional abuse. If the addict had a physically or emotionally ill mother, the therapist must know about the formation of early personality. Unlike the first evaluation criterion, in this area the addict cannot rely on his own sense of the therapist's abilities. The addict can ask recovering friends, his physician, or the therapists in his cocaine treatment program for recommendations and referral to a therapist with expertise in the addict's areas of concern. The addict can also ask several therapists where *they* would go for therapy if they needed it.

When an addict enters individual, group, or family therapy he retains the right to start or stop therapy at any time. The addict should begin therapy with an initial trial period of four to ten weeks. At the end of this time, a decision should be made whether or not to continue. If the patient feels anxious about the therapy, but is assured that the therapist is on to something, he is in the right place. Unrest and anxiety are part of psychotherapy.

Once the patient has worked past the trial period, he should press on. Growth is painful, especially when one is on the verge of a critical change in his inner life. This growth creates pain that often makes the patient feel a need to flee. Termination must be discussed with the therapist; as the addict has learned to trust cocaine treatment and the Twelve Steps, he should work to trust his therapist.

Recovering cocaine addicts are susceptible to certain emotional and personality problems. The problems described in this chapter should not be considered as an exhaustive catalog. If an addict sees himself in these pages, he should talk about it with others. He should decide whether to simply take note of the problem or to proceed ahead with therapy.

Principle 3 — Many cocaine addicts have problems with eating disorders, intimacy, or sexual addiction.

Eating Disorders

It is estimated that twenty-two percent of all female cocaine addicts fulfill the diagnostic criteria for an eating disorder. Eating disorders are more commonly seen in women, but male cocaine addicts have eating disorders more frequently than nonaddicted males. Cocaine produces several desirable effects in people who are prone to develop an eating disorder, including: appetite suppression, increased energy, and a sense of well-being. However, the cocaine crash promotes the opposite symptoms: increased appetite and food binging, decreased energy, and feelings of hopelessness and emptiness. This two-phased effect fuels the development of abnormal food behaviors in a cocaine addict who is prone to develop an eating disorder.

A woman who is prone to develop an eating disorder may try cocaine and experience increased energy and decreased appetite. Later she initiates compulsive food binges, which lead to a weight gain. The weight drives her to diet. While on the diet, she experiments with cocaine, and finds that it helps suppress her appetite and increases her energy. She begins using routinely, and as her cocaine use escalates, she begins to experience more of the cocaine crash. The crash makes her despondent and hungry. The hunger induces additional food binging episodes, creating a vicious cycle.

The most common eating disorder in cocaine-dependent people is bulimia. Bulimia nervosa is an illness typified by discrete binges in which the bulimic consumes large quantities of food, followed by efforts to eliminate the food by purging.

The most common purging behaviors are vomiting or laxative abuse. Other methods of purging include compulsive exercise, water pill abuse, spitting food out, use of enemas, and use of stimulants such as cocaine or thyroid hormones.

As an illness, bulimia typically predates cocaine addiction. It is, therefore, more deeply entrenched than cocaine dependence.

Patients who have a dual problem of cocaine dependence and bulimia nervosa need to arrest both problems in primary treatment. When only one of several addictive behaviors is arrested, the other addictive behaviors grow unchecked. Many women who have bulimia and cocaine addiction enter treatment for cocaine dependence and try to ignore their eating disorder. Eventually, the bulimia initiates a relapse into cocaine use. Let us use an example to describe this problem.

Maureen has been binging and purging by vomiting since age seventeen. She binged and purged at least once a day, sometimes for as long as three hours per day. At twenty, Maureen began using cocaine. She moved from an occasional snort at a party to crack use within two years. While using cocaine, her bulimia seemed to improve, as she only vomited once every two to three weeks. When Maureen turned twenty-six, she landed in drug treatment. She felt shame about her bulimia, and so she did not tell the staff in the cocaine treatment program about her food addiction.

After five weeks of treatment, Maureen returned to work. At first, her bulimia was quiet. Maureen began to think that it had disappeared. One day, under increasing stress at work, Maureen vomited her lunch. Filled with shame, she vowed not to do it again. A week later she ate a large dinner alone, and fell into compulsive food binging. The binge continued for several hours with gorging followed by vomiting. Her bulimia had returned. Although she was upset, Maureen still had a measure of pride because she had not returned to cocaine.

As Maureen attempted to control her bulimia, she gained several pounds. The minor weight problem plagued her. One day in a panic she thought about using cocaine, believing that it would decrease her appetite. After several weeks of deliberation, she went out and bought cocaine—"Only to control my appetite," she rationalized. After one line of cocaine she was filled with anxiety and remorse and promptly rushed back into smoking cocaine. Both of the behaviors of her addictive disease returned, in full relapse. When she smoked cocaine she felt anorectic (not hungry) during Stage I of the Cocaine Addiction Cycle. Then, as she progressed to Stage III, Maureen would binge and purge. Her bulimia and cocaine addition were intertwined into one addiction cycle.

This example describes how an eating disorder, bulimia nervosa, becomes intertwined with cocaine addiction. When using chemicals, the nonchemical addiction often lies dormant. When an addict relapses into one addictive behavior, it promotes relapse in the other. Cocaine addiction is frequently coupled with addictions to food, nicotine, sex, gambling, or spending. Recovery from chemical dependency is always compromised when another facet of the addictive disease goes unchecked.

Treatment for cocaine addiction must be coupled with treatment of other addictions, including eating disorders. Early in treatment, a person with an eating disorder should talk with a therapist or physician. If the therapist is at a loss, a consultation should be requested with a specialist in bulimia and dual addictive illnesses. Once evaluated, both problems must be addressed concurrently.

The first step for a vomiting bulimic is to gain control over vomiting behaviors. Then, the abnormal food behaviors are managed through the use of an *abstinence meal plan,* a consistent regulated pattern of eating that prevents food restriction or binging. An abstinence meal plan is not a diet. It is a way of eating that will grow to encompass abstinence and eventual recovery. Bulimic cocaine addicts should attend a combination of Overeaters Anonymous and Cocaine Anonymous, or Narcotics Anonymous, or Alcoholics Anonymous meetings. A cocaine addict who is also bulimic will need to develop a recovery program that addresses both the food addiction and the chemical dependency.

Difficulties with Intimacy

If an addict has had long-term drug and alcohol problems, he may view interpersonal problems through the distortion created by his addiction. An addict stops maturing emotionally at the age he began drug use. If an addict began using drugs at age twenty, his maturity level will remain that of a twenty year-old as long as he continues to use. If he started drinking and using drugs at age thirteen, he will have the emotional maturity of a thirteen-year-old when he begins recovery; he will start recovery in a second adolescence. Whatever his age when he embarks on recovery, delayed maturity creates interpersonal problems.

Cocaine short-circuits all of an addict's needs for intimacy as well. The need for solace, warmth, and a sense of connection were all directed toward a white powder or a vial of crack. In early recovery, the addict will continue to expect his needs for intimacy to be met as they were while he was using cocaine. He may show little patience for discussion, argument, and compromise.

Intimacy between couples is a learned behavior. Most married addicts need to start their relationships over when one or both of the partners begin recovery. Intimacy occurs when both halves of the relationship learn about each other and work to move past their old modes of relating. Intimacy in recovering couples is best developed in the following three stages:

1. Initial education about how addictive illness affects the addict and coaddict, followed by

2. Individual but parallel growth in recovery from addiction and coaddiction.

3. Not until both halves of the couple have achieved consistent abstinence and strong recovery programs, should they begin intensive couple's therapy to eliminate destructive patterns and develop intimacy.

Whether male or female, recovering cocaine addicts have problems with sexual intimacy. Many addicts combined cocaine and sex and, as a result, have to deal with euphoric recall coloring their memories of sex while under the influence of cocaine. When they are in recovery and understand the mechanism of euphoric recall, addicts remember cocaine-laced sexual incidents in a more rational light. They then report that cocaine hindered as often as it helped their sexual response. Participation in unusual sexual practices during cocaine use produces residual shame or fear. These feelings inhibit intimacy in recovery and are best treated through disclosure in group therapy—preferably in a group designed to handle such issues.

If an addict finds he has problems with sexual intimacy in recovery, using cocaine will only aggravate the problem. In such cases, I recommend marital therapy with a focus on each partner's sexual needs. If the therapist unearths sexual addiction in either partner, it should be treated separately.

Sexual Addiction

Cocaine stimulates the entire brain and decreases one's inhibitions. Part of the brain stimulation produces a sensation of sexual arousal. The combination of an increase in stimulation, heightened sexual arousal, and a decrease in inhibition often propels the addict into unusual sexual behavior. If the addict frequently combines cocaine and sex, he will begin to equate cocaine with sexual activity. Compulsive sex is attached to the compulsive use of cocaine. When cocaine is paired with sex, sexual behavior becomes as compulsive and bizarre as the cocaine behavior. The addict progresses from compulsive and ritualistic sex (in Stage I of the Cocaine Addiction Cycle) to shame and remorse (in Stage III).

Women and, less frequently, men who are cocaine addicted may become "coke whores"—trading sexual favors for free cocaine. Sexual addiction develops as the addict feels the anticipation and excitement of the cocaine and the shame associated with the necessary sexual activity. After the binge, the addict is left with only the shame. Shame serves to further reinforce the addiction. If the excitement/shame cycle continues, it is likely that the coke whore will progress into becoming a full-blown sexual addict.

Sex addicts, on the other hand, may contract cocaine addiction. Some sex addicts experiment with cocaine attempting to extend and heighten their sexual high. If they continue to use cocaine, their casual use grows to addictive use. If a sex addict needs others for pornography, multiple partner sex, voyeurism, or sadomasochistic sex, he or she may use cocaine as bait to catch needed partners. The cocaine bait may turn to hook the provider, engendering a dual addiction to sex and cocaine.

While many sexually addicted men and women are also cocaine addicts, the converse is also true; many cocaine addicted men and women develop compulsive sexual disorders. As a result, it is difficult to tell which addiction is primary, a fact that is ultimately unimportant. It is important, however, to remember that both addictions need to be addressed simultaneously, similar to the concurrent approach developed for the cocaine addict who has an eating disorder. A dual approach prevents one addiction from triggering the other into relapse.

Sexual addicts live in shame. Because sexual addiction creates a deep dishonesty, it may be very difficult for an addict to talk about this part of himself. Nevertheless, a participant in unusual sexual behaviors or compulsive sexual rituals should disclose these behaviors to his therapist. Ideally, the patient will choose to talk to someone with whom he feels safe, so he will be able to talk about himself with rigorous honesty. A knowledgeable therapist will compile a list of the patient's addictive behaviors and use this list to stage the severity of the sexual addiction.[8] Once staged, the therapist can guide his patient to proper simultaneous treatment of the sexual and cocaine addictions.

---

8. See the work of Patrick Carnes. One reference appears in *Additional Readings*.

Emotional Cycling

Principle 4 — Cocaine addicts in recovery suffer from destructive emotional cycles similar to the Cocaine Addiction Cycle.

Patients who recover from cocaine addiction often repeat the Cocaine Addiction Cycle in their sober life. This pattern begins with a slow building of tension and conflict followed by an explosion and a period of tension relief. The following is an example:

> Jeff has been out of treatment for nine months. He feels badly about the financial troubles created by his cocaine addiction, and so he tends to ignore them. He has trouble meeting the mortgage, but feels ashamed and cannot tell his wife. He continues to get overdue notices and warnings from the bank, which he places in a desk drawer at home. As a result, Jeff feels increasing tension and displaces his anger onto his job or into small arguments with his wife. He feels secretive and dishonest about his troubles, and is unable to ask for help. The anxiety builds and he copes by taking on extra work at his job. Soon he is making enough money to meet the mortgage payment. Strangely enough, he still does not pay the mortgage bill. He begins working longer and longer hours. The danger surrounding his mortgage feels uncomfortable but, in another way, it carries a strange excitement.
>
> The tension soon spills over into Jeff's relationship with his wife, generalizing the discord between the two of them. Not paying the bill takes on a larger scope; it is no longer a financial matter. Because he feels guilty about the secret nonpayment, it affects how Jeff relates to his wife. Additionally, his anxiety and shame over this unattended matter motivates him to repress the problem further. Finally, Jeff's wife receives a call from the bank—they are ready to foreclose on the house. Jeff and his wife explode. They argue about his dishonesty. When the argument is complete, Jeff pays the bill and they move to a brief honeymoon period. Jeff's wife begins to feel better about the marriage. She is reassured because he worked extra hours to pay the bill, and attributes his nonpayment to forgetfulness. Jeff, on the other hand, feels restless. Over the next few months, he quits paying the car note. The cycle repeats itself.

Having a marriage that goes through cycles is not unusual. Not paying a bill once in a while is not unusual either. However, the cycle of restlessness that creates unnecessary trouble, which then slowly escalates into a blowup, and is followed by a honeymoon period is a drug-free mirror of the Cocaine Addiction Cycle. This drug-free cycle is known as emotional cycling. It may appear to the outsider that cocaine addicts enjoyed the chaos created by cocaine use, and so they repeat the chaos—without the drug—in recovery. Many recovering cocaine addicts experience the inner restlessness that starts this self-destructive cycle. The cycle stops the restlessness, and places the recovering addict in familiar territory, a territory similar to the emotional cycles that occurred during cocaine use.

Many recovering addicts are bound so deeply in the Cocaine Addiction Cycle that they unconsciously recreate a similar cycle in recovery. Emotional cycling comes from the need to create emotional tension in one's life, and is characterized by ever increasing spirals of anxiety and frustration, followed by an explosion, and relief. The cocaine addict becomes habituated to the cyclic patterns associated with his addiction and, later on in abstinence, he unconsciously repeats these patterns in his interpersonal life.

The therapy for emotional cycling is difficult and deeply intertwined with other issues in recovery. For the therapist, the first order of business is to identify that cycling is present. This may seem hard for the patient to believe. He may think, "I worked long and hard to stop the craziness that cocaine created in my life, and now this therapist is telling me that I'm doing the same thing without cocaine?" Through careful examination, the addict will pick up the pattern of continued emotional sabotage. Once he establishes that the pattern exists, he must systematically remove each of the particular behaviors in order to discourage the slow escalation and the final blowup. This leaves the addict with the underlying anxiety that produced the cycles in the first place. The underlying anxiety, though unnerving, is nothing compared to the devastation caused by the sober binge cycle. One of the most common of these underlying anxieties, a restless inner self, is discussed later in this chapter.

The Oscillating Ego

Principle 5 — Many cocaine addicts have problems with too much or too little ego.

When a person first uses cocaine, he feels "on top of the world" or "in charge of the universe." Then, as his addiction progresses, he begins to feel that life has less meaning. The addict gradually loses his self-respect but cannot share this with others. Cocaine addicts, more than any other type of addict, hide under a facade of ego inflation. They appear self-assured, assertive, and are verbal about their needs. Underneath the external bravado, cocaine addicts suffer from the same problems of low self-esteem as any other type of addict.

Problems of self-esteem are central to addiction. In individual or group therapy, or in support groups, addicts often display a facade of high self-esteem. When this occurs, others may react by saying: "If you feel so good about yourself, why are you here?" In times of brutal self-honesty, this facade breaks down and reveals someone who feels angry, ashamed, and small. The proper treatment for the patient who oscillates between these two ego states is to help him find a healthy middle ground. The addict must be compelled to recognize that he is no more God's gift to mankind than he is the scum of the earth. In some addicts, cocaine has accentuated feelings of omnipotence or impotence extant long before any addiction to cocaine. Whatever its origins, when an addict is honest about his low self-image, he reclaims his knowledge of self.

The sense of camaraderie and fellowship in the twelve-step community is the most powerful medicine for an oscillating ego. By comparing notes and discussing stories, a participant soon feels neither greater than nor less than, but simply part of the recovering community. Cocaine addicts should welcome gentle confrontation from friends, sponsors, or spouses whenever their egos deflate or escalate to extremes.

A healthy ego will develop from involvement in the twelve-step process. If this does not occur, an addict should engage in additional individual or group therapy. Oscillations of ego will arise from time to time in recovery but, given enough time, they will stabilize and the addict will come to know his true self-worth.

Success/Failure Complex

Principle 6 — The success/failure complex is created when cocaine addiction is combined with certain preexisting psychological problems.

Many cocaine addicts are obsessed with success and plagued by failures. Like other addicts, they have an inner sense of failure that stands in stark contrast to their external successes. The tension generated by the conflict between success and failure creates the success/failure complex.

This complex is revealed in many ways. Perhaps it is best illustrated by a clinical example:

> Mark grew up in an upper-middle-class family. His father was a busy man who developed a substantial legal practice. Mark grew up admiring his father, but at a distance. Mark had many physical and intellectual capabilities. His teachers told him that he would do something great with his life, but Mark missed his father. He grew up without paternal advice because his father was focused on building his legal practice. Mark's pride in his father kept him from seeing how angry he was about his father's absence.
>
> When Mark discovered cocaine, he thought he'd found heaven. Over a two year period, he became deeply addicted. When he finally arrived in treatment, for reasons unknown to him he felt incredible anger toward his father, and guilt about his anger. In fact, his denial of his cocaine addiction was enveloped in his conflict about his relationship with his father: "I may use a lot of cocaine, but it is not the primary problem. I came here to settle many things about my life, especially my relationship with my father." I agreed that he had to settle many things. The first issue to settle was that he was an addict and could not use cocaine successfully.
>
> Once out of treatment, Mark found himself trying hard to succeed. He quickly placed his cocaine recovery program below

his need to succeed. He repeatedly relapsed, often just as he was completing a project at work. He described experiencing feelings of seething rage toward his father. *Placing his need to succeed over his recovery guaranteed failure in both endeavors.*

Many father-son dynamics are present in Mark's life. Children internalize messages about their families and remain unaware of most of them. One of Mark's family tapes was that his father was to be the hero, the success of the family. Unknown to Mark, his entire family learned to place the father's achievement in front of any other family needs. In contrast, Mark was told by his family and teachers that he would be a success. He wanted to please his father and do something great with his life. However, to remain a part of his family, Mark could not threaten his father's place as the hero of the family. Therefore, Mark's relationship with his father was based upon him always trying hard, but ultimately failing.

The tension between the spoken message in his family (be a success) and the unspoken family rule (do not outshine your father) established the success/failure complex. Cocaine extended this complex. The contrast between the euphoric reward and the depths of the cocaine crash increase the intensity of Mark's oscillations between success and failure.

Treatment must acknowledge Mark's need to remain in his family. Through individual or, preferably, family therapy, the family agenda of rallying around the father's success must be exposed. Then Mark's father can be seen for what he is, a good man who placed his success before the needs of his family. As a result, he has not been a successful father to his son. This gives Mark the permission to struggle with his present failure—cocaine addiction. Let us continue with another clinical example:

> David grew up in a lower-class family. His family was hard driving, and believed that financial reward was the major indicator of success in life. David felt obligated to do well and studied hard in school. His father and mother spent a great deal of time with him, focusing on his achievements. He was constantly worried about doing the right thing. Among his peers, David was known

as a goody-two-shoes. He attended college and obtained a business degree. Although he fell in love several times, he passed up opportunities to marry, driven to please his parents and succeed in his career.

David went on to succeed financially, but he had many conflicts about his success. He felt guilty for leaving his family behind, despite the fact that they were the ones that drove him to be a financial success. When he went to visit his parents, he was embarrassed by his humble beginnings. His parents hung on his every word and thrilled at his descriptions of the corporate world, but David downplayed his work accomplishments. He felt different from his corporate coworkers, and worked alone.

David moved rapidly up the corporate ladder. When promoted, he would feel a burst of exhilaration. On one of these days, a friend introduced him to cocaine as a way to celebrate. David tried the drug reluctantly and immediately became obsessed. Although the drug exhilarated him in new ways, he described the cocaine crash as somehow familiar. At first, David used only on weekends. He attempted to control his drug use, but soon his cocaine consumption began to affect his work. David's boss noticed that David had changed dramatically. When one of his binges created a crisis at work, his company intervened. They placed him in a cocaine treatment program. David did well in treatment, viewing it as he had school and work—one more area in which to excel. Inside, he felt very angry: "No one has the right to take away my cocaine, the one thing I do for pleasure."

When he was a child, David's family carefully nurtured his drive to succeed. As an adult, it seemed second nature. This drive was not without its costs, as David felt hollow and deprived of other human needs and satisfactions. This lack caused David to believe that, despite all the trappings of success, he had failed at life. Like many cocaine addicts, his ambitious nature prevented him from admitting any failure while, at the same time, this inner sense of failure subconsciously aborted his triumphs. *Thus, he was strung as tightly as a piano wire between two poles: the desire to prevent failure and the constant need to abort his successes.*

The addict who suffers with the success/failure complex can be healed. The psychotherapeutic process is twofold: First, the addict must acknowledge his failures in life. The first failure is the addiction itself. The most important part of recovery for the addict is to recognize his total failure to control his cocaine habit. When the addict denies this absolute inability to control his addiction, he will be forced into a constant battle of control that he cannot win. This battle with chemical dependency exacerbates the preexisting success/failure complex. In therapy, patients need to return to the First Step and its concomitant admission of powerlessness, regardless of how far along they are in recovery. When an addict knows he has failed, he will let go of the battle to control. Knowledge of his powerlessness is paradoxically the crucial step to an addict's fundamental success—recovery. As an addict succeeds in recovery, he paves the way for success in other areas of his life.

Once a deeper understanding of cocaine's control is firmly established, it is time for the addict to review and acknowledge other failures. The critical element is to encourage the addict to view his failures and deficiencies without shame. Shame enlarges envy and hobbles growth. The addict should address his mistakes with sadness and respect, and accept his shortcomings for what they are. A failed marriage, a lost job, a loss of fame and fortune should all be looked at honestly. Psychotherapy is a process that diffuses the effects of shame; as failures are exposed, shame loses its hold. A person who lives with a deep sense of shame leaves the door to addiction open.

Psychotherapy for the success/failure complex must also confront problems with success. The Cocaine Addiction Cycle implants in the addict's mind the belief that every reward is followed by overwhelming loss, grief, and defeat. When cocaine addicts enter recovery, many are afraid of even small successes. Each small reward they experience triggers an association with the powerful reward created by cocaine. This association causes the addict to dread success, fearing that any reward will be followed by despair and anxiety.

To overcome this cascade of negative feelings, an addict must become comfortable with each small triumph and, thus, learn to acknowledge his success. By repeated exposure to and acknowledgment of success, the addict will gradually extinguish the destructive, conditioned cues he has learned to associate with reward. Extinguishing these destructive cues is a process that takes many years but, over time, the intensity of the craving brought on by each subsequent success will grow less and less troublesome.

When the addict has trained himself to extinguish the craving for cocaine that arises from success, his work is half done. Next, with the help of therapy, he should address his underlying fear of success that predates his cocaine addiction. Most cocaine addicts have intense, underlying fears of success that have been generated by:

- An intense drive to succeed—where responsibility is assumed for pulling one's entire family out of a cycle of multi-generational failure.
- Competition with a successful parent—where success is construed as disloyalty.
- Being the *black sheep* in the family. Families develop black sheep by strong unwritten rules. If a black sheep becomes a success, he may be superficially praised, but punished indirectly for straying from his family role.
- A compulsion to succeed that generates a concomitant suppression of hostility toward early parental figures.

When confronted by their fears of success, addicts seem completely unaware of the problem. They say: "Oh, I'm afraid of failure all right. But fear of success?!" The subconscious mind has been sabotaging accomplishments for years. The addict may need to visualize his fear of success by making a repeated survey of his behavior and listening to the evaluation of others.

When an addict has recognized certain failures as his own and come to grips with his fear of success, he will automatically remove himself from the success/failure complex. This does not mean he will be an overnight success. It simply means that he will attain a sense of accomplishment in life and be less prone to sabotage his own success.

Restless Inner Self

Principle 7 — Some addicts in recovery need additional therapy to cope with feelings of restlessness or emptiness.

Many patients in recovery from cocaine addiction are plagued by a sense of inner restlessness. Some people have always been restless and fidgety, and have spent many years attempting to compensate for a feeling of emptiness. If an addict felt restless before he began using cocaine, cocaine use only exacerbated this problem. Although rarely dramatic or overwhelming, this restless inner self can be annoying and relentless. Some addicts relapse just to stop the droning voice inside them. Many addicts remain unaware of this feeling until it is pointed out to them. They have lived with it for so long that they have stopped paying attention to it, unaware that it is jeopardizing their recovery.

The patient who experiences profound feelings of restlessness is treated using a fourfold approach:

1. Initial recognition of restlessness followed by recurrent testing of its intensity.
2. A thorough search of spiritual needs.
3. An exercise plan that includes frequent aerobic exercise.
4. If all this fails, psychotherapy is recommended.

Many patients are relieved when they are able to confront their restless inner self. They have known that something is vaguely wrong, but were unwilling or unable to define the problem. Often, just being able to identify the trouble as something real helps relieve the addict and diminish his sense of emptiness. People who have identified a restless or empty quality within themselves should develop a barometer to gauge the extent of their malaise. The addict should rate this feeling on a scale of 1 to 5 several times a day, and then go over it with his treatment team or therapist. The level of restlessness should be correlated with the level of cocaine craving.

Once a patient has been able to identify the intensity of his inner restlessness, he must develop a plan to reduce it.

To this end, I have found that psychotherapy can be helpful, but not nearly as helpful as spiritual development and exercise. Someone so afflicted should seek to strengthen his relationship with a higher power. Does his spiritual program provide him with a direction in life, a source of calming purpose? If not, he should return to the first three steps, and subsequent study of Step Eleven. The recovering addict should ask a sponsor in his twelve-step group or a spiritual advisor (such as a minister, rabbi, or priest) for help in spiritual matters. If he enjoys the quest, and avoids looking for quick answers, he will have already diminished his restless inner self.

Once the addict's spiritual sense has been awakened, he should consider beginning an exercise program. For anyone over thirty-five or anyone who has a personal or familial history of cardiovascular problems, a thorough physical examination is recommended. Heavy cocaine users, regardless of age or medical history, should also undergo physical examinations before beginning any exercise program, making sure to inform their physicians about the extent of their cocaine habits. If the physician declares that it is safe to exercise, the addict should begin slowly. Many addicts benefit from an evaluation by a physical therapist or exercise specialist; these consultants develop an exercise program suited to the individual's needs. Exercise that is unrewarding or punishing must be avoided. Addicts have suffered enough punishment in the past.

Aerobic exercise is unsurpassed in decreasing inner restlessness. Although depression is harder to shake, this too responds well to exercise and should subside in time.

If a feeling of emptiness continues to plague the addict after careful attention to spiritual needs and physical exercise, psychotherapy is called for. Therapy that unearths past conflicts can be quite disturbing; it is not for the timid. Before entering therapy, the addict's recovery program must be on solid ground.

Feelings of emptiness and restlessness arise from many different psychological problems, and often many blind alleys must be explored before the psychological root of the problem is discovered. In therapy, the patient will probe areas that seem dark and forbidding. Painful issues such as child abuse or parental neglect may surface. The patient may feel at times that therapy serves little meaningful purpose. The patient should be aware that if he feels anxious or emotionally threatened by the therapeutic process, he is getting closer to finding the source of his troubles.

Once unearthed, psychological issues need to be experienced in their entirety. When all the issues have been exhausted in individual therapy, the addict may choose to continue therapy in a group setting or to attend meetings of a specific support group. In a support group, healing will continue and the restless inner self will be replaced by newfound hope and contentment.

Additional Readings for Part Two

Carnes, P. *Contrary to Love: Helping the Sexual Addict*. Minneapolis, MN: CompCare Publishers, 1989.

Cohen, S. *The Chemical Brain: The Neurochemistry of Addictive Disorders*. Irvine, CA: CareInstitute, 1988.

Dackis, C. A., & M. S. Gold. "New Concept in Cocaine Addiction: The Dopamine Depletion Hypothesis." *Neuroscience and Biobehavioral Review*, 9(3): 1-9, 1985.

Hall, W. C., R. L. Talbert, & L. Ereshefsky. "Cocaine Abuse and its Treatment." *Pharmacotherapy*, 10(1):47-65, 1990.

Gold, M. S. & K. Verebey. "The Psychopharmacology of Cocaine." *Psychiatric Annals*, 14:714-23, 1984.

Marlatt, G. A., & J. R. Gordon. *Relapse Prevention: Maintenance Strategies in the Treatment of Addictive Behaviors*. New York, NY: Guilford Press, 1985.

Smith, D. E., & D. R. Wesson. *Treating the Cocaine Abuser*. Center City, MN: Hazelden Foundation, 1985.

Smith, D. E. "Cocaine-alcohol Abuse: Epidemiological, Diagnostic and Treatment Considerations." *The Journal of Psychoactive Drugs*, 18(2):117-129, 1986.

Spitz, H. H., & J. S. Rosecan. *Cocaine Abuse: New Directions in Treatment and Research*. New York, NY: Brunner/Mazel, 1987.

Tennant, F. S., Jr., & A. A. Sagherian. "Double-blind Comparison of Amantadine and Bromocriptine for Ambulatory Withdrawal from Cocaine Dependence." *Archives of Internal Medicine*, 147(1):109-12, 1987.

Wallace, B. C. "Psychological and Environmental Determinants of Relapse in Crack Cocaine Smokers." *Journal of Substance Abuse Treatment*, 6:95-106, 1989.

Washton, A. M. *Cocaine Addiction, Treatment, Recovery, and Relapse Prevention*. New York, NY: W.W. Norton & Company, 1989.

Index

A

"A little bit won't hurt", 129
A.A. "Big Book"
    See "Big Book"
Abscess, 20
Abstinence violation effect, 143-144
    See also Relapse prevention
Acquired Immunodeficiency Syndrome, 43
Aftercare
    See Continuing care
Agitation, 11, 39, 54-55, 100
Alcohol, xii, xiv, 17, 23, 37-38, 47, 49, 51-52, 54, 57, 92, 94, 97, 103, 106, 108-109, 114-115, 117, 124-125, 131-139, 141-146, 151, 154
Alcoholics Anonymous, xiv, xvii, 43-44, 51-52, 113-114, 154
Alcoholism, xiv, 33, 43-44, 136
Alkaline plug, 5
"All this time I was fooling myself", 141
Alprazolam, 37
Alveoli, 14, 21
Amantadine, 65-66, 169
Amino acids, 67-68
    See also L-phenylalanine, L-tryptophan, and L-tyrosine
Anger, 108-112, 145, 158, 161
Anhedonia, 39, 70, 72, 74, 107
Anhedonic depression, 70, 107-108, 131
Animal
    instincts, 88-89
    research, 27, 133
Antibiotics, 16
Anxiety, 38, 61, 77, 79-80, 107, 150-151, 153, 158-159, 164
Arterial blood, 10, 15
Auditory hallucinations, 26, 61
Authority figures, 26
Automatic movements, 61

AVE
　See Abstinence violation effect
Avoiding negative situations, 130
　See also Relapse prevention
Axon, 56, 58

B

Baboons, 28
Bacteria, 16, 20
Balanced diet, 68, 130-131
Bank
　automatic teller card, 128
　direct deposit, 128
Barbiturates, 37
"Become friends with your feelings", 112
Behavioral techniques, 127-128
　See also Relapse prevention
"Better living through chemistry", 8
Between cocaine binges, 39
"Big Book", xiv, xvii, 114
Bilirubin, 17
Black sheep, 165
Blood-brain barrier, 14-15
Body temperature, 5, 25, 38, 71
Body thermostat, 25
Brain
　breathing center, 25
　cocaine naive brain, 61
　medial prefrontal cortex, 29
Bromocriptine, 65-66, 169
Bronchitis
　See Chronic bronchitis
Brutal self-honesty, 160
Bulimia Nervosa, 131, 152-154

C

C.A.
 See Cocaine Anonymous
Caffeine, 6
Cancer, 18-19, 67
Carbamazepine, 24, 69-70
Cardiac standstill
 See Heart standstill
Career path, 137
Cash, 40, 129, 138
"Change is the real work of recovery", xii, 50
Changing jobs, 129
Chest pain, 29, 36, 90-91
 See also Heart
Children of an addict, 100, 109, 111
Chlordiazepoxide, 37
Chronic bronchitis, 21
Circadian rhythms, 130
Cirrhosis, 17, 23
 See also Liver
Coaddiction, 155
Coca, 4-5, 7
 See also Cocaine
Cocaine
 Addiction Cycle, 3, 27, 32-35, 37, 39-42, 48-49, 52, 62, 72, 77, 79, 82, 92-93, 98, 104, 110, 117, 122, 130, 141, 144, 148, 154, 156, 158-159, 164
 alkaloids of, 4
 body packing, 15
 casual use of, xii, 48, 133
 Cocaine Anonymous, 51-52, 113, 154
 complications from use, 13, 15, 17, 19, 21, 23, 25, 27, 29, 31
 dealing, 8, 40, 87, 128
 depression, 72
 effects on the body, 14
 effects on the mind, 25
 euphoria, 4, 10-11, 81, 85, 91, 103
 grandiosity, 39, 73-74, 88, 97, 99, 119
 history of use, 4-5, 7, 9, 11

Cocaine *(continued)*
    lights, 36
    oral ingestion, 15
    paraphernalia, 86, 128
    pre-cocaine jitters, 41, 79
    romancing, 88, 99
    seizures, 24, 62
    tapes in the brain, 76
    treatment programs, 151, 153, 163
    was once declared to be nonaddicting, 7, 27, 54
    withdrawal from, 53-54, 66, 69-70, 72
Cocaine Recovery Workbook, The, xiv, xvii-xviii, 34, 49, 75, 85, 91, 94, 96, 98, 101, 110, 114, 118, 120, 122, 125, 127, 132, 145
Cognitive
    distortions, 88
    techniques, 127, 132
Coke whore, 156
Condoms, 15, 19
Conflicts about success, 163
    See also Fear of success
Confrontation, xiv, 94, 160
Conscious knowledge, 32
Continuing care, 137, 147, 149-150
Convulsions
    See Seizures
Coping response, 140, 142, 145-146
Coworkers, 100, 163
Crack, 6, 8, 10-11, 14-15, 21-22, 24, 33, 85, 153, 155, 169
    See also Cocaine
    dealer, 8
    smoking, 6, 14, 21
Craving
    conditioned-cue, 84
    covert, 82
    management techniques, 80, 126-127
    overt interoceptive, 78
    reinforced-use, 25-26, 77-78, 141

Crescendo of anticipation, 90
Cyanocobalamin
   See Vitamins
Cyclic use pattern
   See Cocaine Addiction Cycle

D

Dackis, Charles, 64-65, 169
Dalmane, 37
Death, 16, 22, 28, 83, 89
Decreased appetite, 152
Dehydration, 89
Dementia, 19
Denial, xiii, 30-31, 70, 88, 91-98, 133, 148, 161
Depression, 25, 27, 31, 54-55, 61, 63-64, 69-70, 72-73, 76,
   100, 103-105, 107-109, 111, 131, 167
   See also Cocaine depression
Detoxification, 23, 47, 53-57, 59, 61, 63-69, 71-73, 91, 113
Diazepam, 37
Dietitian, 131
Dissonance conflict, 140
   See also Relapse prevention
Doctor
   See Physician
Dopamine, 59-60, 63-68, 70, 169
   See also Neurotransmitter
   receptors, 63, 65
Dope fiend, 7
Drug
   "drugs fix drug addiction", 55
   hot lines, 39
   modulator drugs, 37-39, 96
   romancing, 80-81, 101
   screens, use in recovery, 147
   seeking behavior, 40
Dysphoria, 11, 26, 104, 107

E

Early cocaine crash
    See Cocaine Addiction Cycle, Stage I
Eating disorders, 90, 96, 148, 152, 154
    See also Bulimia Nervosa
EMIT-RIA
    See Drug screens, use in recovery
Emotion
    cycling, 159
    emotional baggage of the past, 149
    roller coaster of, 106
Endocarditis, 16
Eosinophilia-myalgia, 68
Erythroxylon coca, 4
Erythroxylon novogranatense, 4
Ethanol, 22
Ethyl ether, 21
Euphoric recall, 99
Examination, physical, 167
Exercise, xiv, xvii-xviii, 29, 34, 73, 75, 79-80, 93, 95, 98,
    101, 110, 114, 120, 125, 130-133, 145, 149, 153, 166-167
    aerobic, 73, 131, 166-167
    compulsive, 153

F

False sense of security, 41, 98
Family, 22, 43, 81, 100, 105, 107, 116, 151, 161-163, 165
Fear of success, 165
Feeling cured in recovery, 82
Feelings
    inner restlessness, 159, 166-167
    of emptiness, 39, 166-167
Fight or flight reaction, 90
Finances, xii, 30, 100, 105, 158, 162-163
Flu-like syndrome, 18
Flurazepam, 37

Folic acid
   See Vitamins
Fork in the road, 40
Freud, Sigmund, 5, 43
Friends, new set of, 137

G

Gambling, 96-97, 125, 154
Gastrointestinal distress, 41
God, 39, 119-121, 160
Gold, Mark, 43-44, 64-65, 169
Gordon, Judith, 138, 169
Grandiosity, 39, 72-74, 88, 97, 99, 119
Grief, 51, 108-109, 111, 164
Group psychotherapy
   See Psychotherapy, group

H

Halikas, James, 69
Harrison Act, 7
Heart
   attack, 22, 29, 36, 90, 131
   palpitations, 22
   rate, 5, 22
   rhythm disturbances, 21-22
   standstill, 22, 36
   surgery, 16
Hepatitis
   hepatitis A, 17
   hepatitis B, 17
   hepatitis C, 17
   virus causing, 17-18, 23
High-risk situation, 139-140, 142, 144-146
   See also Relapse prevention
Hoarseness, 21
Hobbies, 107, 136
Homicide, 27

Honeymoon period, 158-159
Human Immunodeficiency Virus, 18
    HIV Antibody Titre, 19-20
Hunger, 38, 61, 90, 152
    lack of, 61

I

"I'm here to stop cocaine, not to deal with other things", 96
"I don't want to change anything else", 49
"I just found myself in a bar with a drink in my hand", 126
"I might as well give up and use now", 89
"I'll never do this again", 39
"I'm thinking just fine now", 120
Immune system, 18-19
Incan Empire, 4
Incidence of addiction, 7
Instincts, 88-91, 151
    changes in, 89
    instinctual brain, 89, 91
Insufflation, 14-15, 32
Intercourse, difficulties with, 26
Intimacy, difficulties with, 154
Intravenous
    injection, 7, 16
    use, 14

J

Job location, 128, 136
"Just one hit won't hurt", 140

K

Kaposi's sarcoma, 18
Kidneys, 16, 67

L

L-phenylalanine, 65, 67-68
L-tryptophan, 68
L-tyrosine, 65, 67-68

Laboratory research, 13
Late Crash
    See Cocaine Addiction Cycle, Stage III
Laxative abuse, 153
Leisure, 30, 125, 130-131, 134
    leisure activities, 30, 130-131, 134
    leisure plan, 131
Librium, 37
"Life is dull after cocaine", 91
Life threatening complications, 53-54, 75, 89-90
Lifestyle
    modification techniques, 127
Liver, 13, 17, 23, 67
    inflammation, 17
Loneliness, 108-112
Lorazepam, 37
Low self-esteem, 97, 131, 160
Lungs, 10, 14-16, 20-21
    damage to, 21
    mediastinum of, 21
Lymphoma, 19

M

Marijuana, 8, 38, 49, 96
Marlatt, Alan, 138, 169
Medical textbooks, 7
Messenger chemicals
    See Neurotransmitters
Minister, 167
Money, large sums of, 78, 128, 136
Monkey, 28-29, 32
    See also Rhesus monkeys
Mood problems, 55, 70, 113
Morphine addiction, 5
Motor
    acceleration, 61
    tics, 61
Mucous membrane, 14-15

Muscle
    calf muscles, 22
    increased tone, 61-62
    jaw muscles, 22
    muscle cramping, 23, 61
    muscle twitching, 23
    myalgias, 18, 68
Myocardial infarction
    See Heart attack

N

N.A.
    See Narcotics Anonymous
Narcotics, 7, 23, 37-38, 106, 125
Narcotics Anonymous, xiv, xvii, 44, 51-52, 113-114, 154
Nasal
    passages, 9, 15-16
    septum, 15-16
Nausea, 17, 65
Needle sharing, 18
Nerve cell
    See Neuron
Neurochemistry of cocaine, 57
Neuron, 53, 56-66, 70
  axon of, 56, 58
    postsynaptic, 58-59
    presynaptic, 58, 63, 66
Neurotransmitter, 57-60, 63-67, 107
    reuptake of, 59-63, 66, 68
Niacin
    See Vitamins
Nicotine, 96-97, 125, 154
Nieman, Albert, 5
Nightclub, 136
Norepinephrine, 59-60, 63-68, 70
    See also Neurotransmitter

O

Oscillating ego, 160
Overdose
    inadvertent, 26
    intentional, 27

P

Pacing the floor, 37, 61
Pain, 22, 29, 51, 90-92, 109, 111, 151
    avoidance, 90
Painful truth about ourselves, 92
Paradoxes in recovery, 116
Paradoxical dysphoria, 104
Paranoia, 11, 26, 36, 61, 100
Parents, 26, 100, 109, 150, 163
Parlodel, 65
Partial day treatment, 99
    See also Treatment
Partial seizures
    See Seizures
"Party is over", 133
Patent medicine industry, 6-7
Paycheck, direct deposit of, 128-129
Payday binge, 129
Peer group, 111
    See also Friends, new set of
Personality, formation of early traits, 151
Phrases
    "A little bit won't hurt", 129
    "All this time I was fooling myself", 141
    "Better living through chemistry", 8
    "Change is the real work of recovery", xii, 50
    "Cocaine is more powerful than you", 116
    "I don't want to change anything else", 49
    "I just found myself in a bar with a drink in my hand", 126
    "I won't turn out like my customers", 135
    "I'll never do this again", 39
    "I'm thinking just fine now", 120

Phrases *(continued)*
 "Just one hit won't hurt", 140
 "Life is dull after cocaine", 91
 "The party is over", 133
 "This cocaine was not strong enough", 35
 "This time I will have a little better control", 35
 "This treatment stuff does not look hard", 97
 "Why did I do that again?", 51
 "Will I ever relapse?", 138
Physician, xiii, xvii, 5, 19, 42, 54, 71, 91, 106, 108, 121, 131, 135, 150-151, 154, 167
Pink cloud, 106-107
Pneumomediastinum, 21
Pneumonia, 19, 21
Pornography, 157
Positive behaviors
 See Relapse prevention
Power greater than ourselves, 118-119
Powerlessness, 116-117, 119, 164
Process model
 See Relapse prevention
Psychologists, xiii
Psychotherapy, 48, 51, 73, 108-109, 124, 148-151, 164, 166-167
 group, 48, 109
 long-term, 48
 therapist in, xvii, 42, 148, 150-151, 154, 156-157, 159, 166-167
Pure Food and Drug Act, 7
Purging, 152-153
Pyridoxine
 See Vitamins

R

Rapid disorganized thought, 61
Rapid speech, 61
Rational mind, 29-30, 38
Reading, additional, 20, 33, 43, 64, 66, 90, 157, 169
Recovery residence, 48, 141, 143
Recovery, path of, 47, 52, 91, 113-114, 122, 126

Relapse
    components of, 139
    definition of, 125
    example of, 141
    road to, 126-127, 138-139, 144
Relapse contracts
    See Relapse prevention
Relapse prevention
    points of intervention in, 144
    positive behaviors, 130, 132
    process model, 126, 138, 143
    seemingly irrelevant decision, 139, 141-142, 144-145
    use of contracts in, 124
Remorse, xiii, 27, 36, 38-39, 72, 100, 104, 153, 156
Resentments, 51, 109-110
Restless
    inner self, 159, 166-168
Retrograde amnesia, 24
Reuptake
    economy, 63
    pump, 59-63, 68
Reward
    center, 10, 29-30, 53, 60-61, 65, 89, 100, 107
    sensation of, 11, 61, 107
Rhesus monkeys, 28
Rhythm disturbances
    See Heart
Riboflavin
    See Vitamins

S

Sadness, 103, 108, 111-112, 145, 164
Safe sex practices
    See Sex, safe practices of
Sanity, 118-120
Scarring of the skin, 20
Sedatives, 23, 37-38, 54-55, 106
Seemingly irrelevant decision, 139, 141-142, 144-145
    See also Relapse prevention

Seizure, 16-17, 24-26, 29, 36, 54, 61-63, 69, 90-91, 93
  See also Cocaine seizure
  grand mal, 62
  kindling, 24, 63
  partial, 62
Self
  attribution of self, 140-141, 143
  deprecatory thoughts, 39
  efficacy, 142
      See also Relapse prevention
  self-abuse, 110
Semen, 18
Septic infection, 16
Serotonin, 60, 63-64, 66-68, 70
Sex
  multiple partner, 157
  safe sex practices, 18, 20
Sexual
  abuse, 51, 111
  addiction, 90, 148, 152, 156-157
  behaviors, unusual, 157
  contact, 17-18
  drive, 90
  intimacy, 155-156
  orgasm, 26
  transmission, 17-18
Shame, 27, 39, 104, 110, 122, 127, 142, 151, 153, 156-158, 164
SID
  See Relapse prevention, seemingly irrelevant decision
Simple sugars, 131
Sleep
  erratic pattern, 130
  induction center, 62
  patterns, unusual, 62
  proper amount, 130
Sleeplessness, 61
Slogans
  See Phrases
Smith, Dr. Bob, 51

Sober life, 158
Social workers, xiii
Spiritual
    experience, 47, 50-51
    life, xii, 47, 50-51, 55, 120, 133, 139, 149, 166-167
    program, 167
Spouse, 30, 100, 111, 128-130, 146
    who is addicted, 128
Stages of the Cocaine Addiction Cycle
    Stage I, 27, 34-35, 37-42, 49, 62, 68, 72-73, 77, 79, 82, 98, 104, 122, 154, 156
    Stage II, 27, 34, 38-39, 42, 49, 62, 68, 72, 98, 104, 154, 156
    Stage III, 27, 34, 38-39, 42, 62, 68, 104, 154, 156
    Stage IV, 34-35, 39-40, 42, 72-73, 79, 82, 122
    Stage V, 35, 40-41, 79, 84, 93, 97
Step work takes time, 122
Steps of recovery
    Step One, 113, 115-118, 122
    Step Study, 114
    Step Three, 113, 120-121
    Step Two, 113, 118-120
Subconscious mind, 134-135, 139, 165
Success, fear of, 165
Success/Failure Complex, 161
Suicide, 27, 39, 108
Symmetrel, 65-66
Symptom, 91, 124-125
    of addiction, 124-125
Synapse, 57, 59, 63
    cleft of, 57-58, 60, 63
Synchronous electrical discharges
    See Seizure
Syringes, shared, 17
    See also Needle sharing
Systematic exposure, 86
    See also Relapse prevention

T

Tachycardia, 5
Tegretol, 24, 69
Therapy
    See Psychotherapy
Thiamine
    See also Vitamins
Thought acceleration, 61
Tics, 23
Time, distortion of, 38
Tolerance, 26, 30, 61, 103
Trachea, 21
Transformation, 42, 51-52, 115, 122
Trauma of being addicted, 40, 50-51, 92, 94, 101, 107-108, 150-151
Treatment
    centers, 39, 53, 68, 114
    residential, 99
Tricyclic antidepressants, 69, 71
Trust, 84, 91, 119, 121, 150-151
Twelve Steps and Twelve Traditions, xiv, xvii, 44, 114, 123
Twelve Steps, literature of, 114

U

Uber Coca, 5
Unmanageability, 117-119
Using in isolation, 26

V

Valium, 37
Vasculitis, 20
Venous system, 9, 14
Vicious cycle, 79, 122, 141, 152
    See also Cocaine Addiction Cycle
Viruses, 16-18, 20, 23
Vitamin C, 64-65, 68-69
    See also Vitamins

Vitamins
- B12, Cyanocobalamin, 69
- deficiencies caused by cocaine use, 64, 68
- folic acid, 64, 68-69
- niacin, 69
- riboflavin, 69
- thiamine, 64, 69
- vitamin C, 64-65, 68-69

Voice problems, 21
Vomiting, 17, 65, 153-154
Voyeurism, 157
- *See also* Sexual behaviors, unusual

W

Water pill abuse, 153
Ways of thinking, 126, 132
Welcome to recovery, 123
Western Blot, 19
"Why can't I tell them about my past?", 142
"Why did I do that again?", 51
"Why do I feel a sense of reward?", 84
"Will I ever relapse?, 138
Wilson, Bill, 51
Wishing to feel happy, 104
Withdrawal, complications of, 54
- *See also* Cocaine withdrawal

Witnessed urine drug screens
- *See* Drug screens, use in recovery

Work, missing, 36
Worst cocaine nightmare, 101

X

Xanax, 37

About the Author

Paul H. Earley is a physician who specializes in the treatment of chemical dependency and eating disorders. He is the Medical Director of the CounterPoint Center of CPC Parkwood Hospital, an addiction treatment program that treats chemical dependency, eating disorders, and nicotine dependence. He directs the Impaired Professionals Program at CPC Parkwood Hospital. He is the President of the Georgia Chapter of the American Society of Addiction Medicine, a certified addiction medicine specialist and an active member of the American Society of Addiction Medicine. Dr. Earley is a dynamic speaker and educator. He lives in Atlanta with his wife and two children.